STREET VIEW
THE DYING OF AMERICAN CITIES

MARILYN RIBEIRO

HARBOR CITY
READING, PA

STREET VIEW
The Dying of American Cities

Copyright©2020 Marilyn Ribeiro

All Rights Reserved

ISBN 978-1-7359695-0-3

Published by Harbor City, 2020

Reading, PA

For All Americans

CONTENTS

INTRODUCTION 9

1 YESTERDAY AND TODAY 12

2 EDUCATION 21

3 OUR FAILING SCHOOLS 39

4 EMPLOYMENT 46

5 IMMIGRATION.. 58

6 MIGRATION... 68

7 HOMELESSNESS.. 83

8 THE DRUG EPIDEMIC 88

9 CRIME.. 116

10 SEXUAL ASSAULT...................................... 124

11 CHILD ABUSE 138

12 DISABILITY.. 154

13 MENTAL ILLNESS 164

14 HEALTHCARE.. 191

15 THE GIFT OF LIFE 213

16 SOCIAL PROGRAMS 216

17 THE COST OF INHERITANCE TAX......... 228

18 A CULTURE OF ANGER AND HATE 240

19 RACISM 264

20 WHAT MAKES A LEADER......................... 284

ACKNOWLEDGEMENTS 298

INTRODUCTION

The Nacirema are a north American group living in the territory between Canadian Cree the Yaqui and Tarahumare of Mexico and the Carib ad Arawak of the Antilles. Little is known of their origin although tradition states that they come from the east.

Nacirema culture exists in a highly developed economic society where its people spend much time in economic pursuits as well as ritual activity. Much of the rituals have to do with the human bodies, health and appearance.

Barbaric practices are common such as women baking their heads in ovens, and men scraping the surfaces of their faces with a razor. Both have an obsession with seeing a holy mouth man once or twice a year who exercise evils from their mouths with a variety of tools such as augers, awls, and probes, a torturous procedure. Every day the tribe members insert hog hair brushes into their mouths using a vigorous motion.

These people go to temples known as latipso where they receive very harsh treatment. They are forced to lie on hard beds for hours and receive ceremonial treatment which involves discomfort and torture. They are forced to eat substances which are supposed to heal them. These ceremonies may not heal them and may even kill them.

I first heard of the Nacirema in my 7th grade social studies class. My teacher read this to our class and gave us a homework assignment to write an essay on our opinion of this lifestyle and we would discuss our opinions the next day in class. She asked us to think about whether or not we would be open to visit or even try this lifestyle.

The next day all thirty-three students in the class unanimously agreed that we would never want anything to do with this culture. For the entire class time we all had a turn at stating what our written opinions were and we all agreed we would never want to visit a country like this let alone live in it. Some students said that we should immediately try to rescue the victims of this culture and allow them to live in our country where they would be treated in a more humane manner.

The teacher asked us what bothered us the most about this culture. Many of us seemed to be bothered about the ceremonious temples where people were forced to lie on hard beds and receive abusive treatment that may kill them. Someone suggested that we send military troops in to bomb these temples.

The teacher suggested something to the class that seemed outrageous. She asked us if it ever occurred to us that the members of this tribe may not want to be rescued at all. After all, this was the only lifestyle ever known to them and maybe they were happy. None of us could really imagine this and none of us were open to remotely considering it.

Much to everyone's shock in the classroom that day, the teacher broke the news to us that we are living in this culture every day. Nacirema is American spelled backwards. Woman baking their heads in ovens is describing women sitting under hairdryers. Men scraping their faces with razors describes men shaving. Hog hair brushes are toothbrushes and holy mouth men are dentists. The holy shrines referred to as latipso are hospitals spelled backwards, dropping the "h".

This was a writing by Horace Mitchell Miner and published in 1956 describing the culture in the United States of America. This exercise took our minds out of the familiarity of our own culture as if we had never experienced it and gave us sight, into a culture we all knew so well but seeing it from an entirely different perspective. This can also work in reverse where an entire population can be encouraged to see a flawed culture in a positive light that they believe should continue.

It was proven in that classroom that all thirty-three students without experiencing a culture from the street view, it is possible to have no recognition of one's own culture. It proves that a culture could possibly experience great changes over a period of time without awareness, taking a whole society down a very dark path to a society so flawed without ever realizing it until it is too late or never realizing it at all.

1

YESTERDAY AND TODAY

June 1962

I was a bird, a bee, a fairy, or anything else that could fly as I burst through the side door of the tiny house I lived in with my parents. It seemed like an eternity since I awoke that morning in the tiny bedroom next to the window facing my backyard. Everyday started the same way with the sound of the train whistle off in the distance. It would still be dark outside as I lay in my bed and slowly watched the sky out my window, turn a variety of shades of gray before daylight. One morning I got out of my bed, got fully dressed, went downstairs and out the side door. My imagination took over as the trees in the yard and the flowers in the garden came alive. I looked up to see my father briskly walking towards me. "What do you think you are doing out here at this hour?" he seemed to shout and whisper at the same time. I knew it had something to do with the dangers of kidnapping. It always seemed like an eternity, when my father appeared at the doorway of my bedroom in the daylight to tell me I could get up. I would follow him downstairs as he tied his tie and then we would eat breakfast. After breakfast he and every father in the neighborhood of tiny Cape Cod homes, left to go to their jobs. I sat patiently at the kitchen table in my seat next to the side door for my mother to come downstairs to the tiny kitchen. I loved my backyard in the morning when everything was so still and the air was so fresh. I had a sandbox, a swing set, and a picnic table that our neighbor had given us. My father had sanded it and painted it until it looked new. My mother planted beautiful flower gardens along the backyard property line. I would play for hours in my backyard, until the other kids in the neighborhood would start to come out later in the morning. The boy across the street and the boy next door, both a year younger would come out first. I would sit on their porches while they ate their cereal and then we would ride up and down the street on our go carts. They both had sisters older than me and at night after dinner we would jump rope in the street. In the afternoon, I'd walk down the street and play with three girls my age.

That morning the dew glistened in the grass in front of me as the sun behind me warmed my back. The smell of my new summer clothes accompanied the wonderful fresh air smells of the earth all around me. The promise of an early summer beautiful day was imminent. I ran as fast as I could, past my mother's flower garden, adding another new fresh smell. I jumped on my swing set and began to swing as fast as I could with my feet in front of me. Much to my dismay, I realized that the toes of my new navy blue Keds were wet from the dew in the grass. I was upset with myself because I would now have to live with my wet feet for the rest of the day. I was swinging back and forth, frowning at my wet sneakers when suddenly over the tops of my sneakers I saw something I had never seen not even on TV. Three police cars glided slowly past my house. Two parked in the street in front of the house next door and one in their driveway. Six policemen hesitantly got out of the police cars and surrounded the house next door. The police officer who drove the car into the driveway took out a megaphone as he nodded to the others within eyesight. The guns that rested in their holsters looked different than the ones we played cops and robbers with. Through the megaphone I heard the police officer request that the man next door come out of the house with his hands up. I slowly slid off the swing and walked towards them to get a closer look at the guns. My mother stood on the side porch calling me to come into the house. Bill Sommers, the neighbor, stepped out of his house with his hands up. Three of the police officers surrounded him as I watched them handcuff him while reading him his rights. I ran towards the side porch and into the side door past my mother. She led me into the playroom off the kitchen and shut the door. I was about to go to the side window where I would have a good view of what I had just left when the play room door flew open and my mother marched in and over to that window. She briskly pulled the Venetian blind down and ordered me not to go anywhere near the window. She retreated back out of the room and closed the door. The sound of Bill Sommers arrest moved to the front of the house. I could hear the police on their walkie talkies and their car doors slam. My step stool was by the front window and I was tempted to go take a look, but I knew that my mother would be mad if she came back in and caught me doing what she just told me not to do. I sat down on the floor and picked up my paper dolls. The new McCall's magazine had come in the mail the day before along with the new summer outfits that I had already cut out for Betsy McCall. Bill Sommers had just been arrested for the third time since my parents had moved into the house next door five years ago. He was the only father who did not leave at 8:00am every morning with the other fathers for work. Unemployment and crime did not exist in any neighborhood that I grew up in. The fact that Bill Sommers was home every day was so odd, it had the whole neighborhood trying to guess how he supported a wife and four kids. What made this family odder yet, was that they had a new Cadillac in the driveway, a colored TV, and a finished basement. These items were considered luxuries that no one living in this lower middle-class neighborhood could afford. Every time Bill Sommers was arrested, his wife, Ruthie, would come over and have tea with my mother. They would talk about everything under the sun but what he did for a living, and his arrest because no one talked about things like that back then.

November 2014

It was 5:00pm as I drove into a neighborhood that had been crime ridden for a very long time. Employment did not exist for anyone on this block, but only crime and blight. It was already dark, not a neighborhood you wanted to be in after dark but I felt safe because of the police presence. There were three police cars surrounding the corner property next door to my building and the yard was swarming with police in bullet proof vests. I parked in the parking space in front of the house across the street and watched for a minute. One of the police officers was standing in the middle of the commotion with an assault rifle pointed towards the sky. All the other officer's guns were still positioned in their holsters. I calculated that as long as I had my key ready, I could quickly run across the street, unlock the security door, and be inside before any shooting could possibly start. I made a run for it and as soon as I got inside, I ran straight up the flight of stairs and knocked on the door. There was music playing louder than usual so I knocked again, figuring they may not have heard the first knock. A teenage girl answered the door and motioned to the hallway inside the apartment with a bedroom door at the end of it. I walked down the hall and knocked on the door. A woman's voice told me to come in. As I opened the door, I held up my receipt book to motion that I was there to collect rent. A man and woman lay in bed watching TV. The woman got up pulling a sheet around her and started to look through dresser drawers. She pulled cash from several different places and as she was pulling it together, I asked them if they were aware that the house next door was surrounded by the police. There were two windows in the bedroom facing the commotion next door with the obvious flashing of lights on squad cars. They were indifferent to it. I gave them a receipt and left. As I walked by the crime scene on the way out, I noticed about twenty or so assault rifles that had been confiscated from the house next door laying on a table as several of the police officers examined them. The house was vacant but apparently there had been evidence that the house was being inhabited. That was nothing unusual as every vacant house was eventually taken over and mostly by people here in this country illegally. I realized that the raid of this house was prompted by the shooting I had witnessed just a week ago while doing a minor roof repair from above. A large van parked in front of my building right below me, pulled out of the parking spot and up to the property across the street moving very slowly and then stopped. The van door opened and shots were fired from inside at a young man sitting on the porch before speeding away. The young man was lying on the sidewalk and screaming that he had been shot. I had often nodded and said good morning to the people who would get out of this van some mornings after parking it in front of my three-unit apartment building. The van was a larger one about ten to fifteen years old with a variety of bumper stickers saturating the back. Most of the stickers were from southwest states as well as south of the border. I smiled and greeted them every morning and sometimes they would return the greeting in Spanish. It began to make sense as I realized these people were controlling the drug trade on the block and the next block up. There had been many shootings on this block as well as the block before and after. A six-year old child had been killed the previous year, the victim of a crossfire in a drive by shooting as she sat on the front porch of her home. The day of the shooting I witnessed from the roof, at least twenty people sitting outside grilling on little hibachi grills and playing cards. Someone called the police from their cell phone and shortly police and ambulances arrived. Everyone then went back to what they were doing. The story later reported was very different than what happened. The van was never mentioned but it was reported that someone walking by in a hoodie pulled a gun and shot the guy and kept walking. The residents on the block lived off disability income and purchased drugs from the people in the van. They did not give an accurate report to the police because they either felt a sense of loyalty or were afraid of retaliation. I never saw the van or the people again. No one was brought to justice for that shooting and the story was never referred to in the news again.

During my childhood, industries had their ups and downs, but for the most part if you worked for a company that was having the downs, another job was easy to find. Bill Sommers would be considered unemployed and unemployment did not exist in neighborhoods where people owned homes. That was impossible because of the government controls on mortgages requiring employer documentation. Criminal activity excludes criminals from homeownership and puts them primarily in low income rental housing. Ruthie grew up in a wealthy neighborhood while Bill grew up in the inner city. Ruthie's mother was the real owner of the home that they lived in.

Bill Sommers had been arrested for running an illegal betting operation. He was not a violent criminal nor did he bring them home with him. He and his wife were very nice neighborly respectful people. Their children played with the other children in the neighborhood never causing any problems. On the day of his arrest my mother was not worried about me getting caught in any possible gunfire and I'm sure that never crossed her mind. She did not want me to witness the neighbor being arrested as people didn't talk about those things back then.

The above two stories happened fifty-two years apart and clearly represent not only the difference in criminals but also demonstrate the desensitization of our society. Over those past decades we have witnessed complications in our society that have brought extreme stress into people's lives. We have seen technology changes as well as manufacturing companies going out of business leaving the employees unemployed and untrained to do anything else. Some are resourceful and become trained to do something else and many give up. Even though an employee was able to get training and find something else, it was at a fraction of the salary that he earned before causing him to downsize in lifestyle considerably. Along with the employment problems, home prices escalated and sometimes quickly leaving many unable to buy homes. In the early 1980's, we saw double digit interest rates, and different mortgage programs to help people become homeowners such as the adjustable mortgage. Following that was the beginning of looser lending requirements such as lower down payments and increased lending ratios. Less money down means a higher monthly mortgage payment taking away more monthly income. We saw daycare centers spring up so that women could go back to work and contribute to the expenses. We saw home equity lines of credit to solve the problems of repairs needed that homeowners couldn't afford any other way except through another monthly payment. The stress caused by unemployment and housing caused symptoms such as a high divorce rate, a high number of bankruptcy filings, child abuse, elderly abuse, animal abuse, drug and alcohol abuse, violent crime and non-violent crime, mental illness, homelessness, and school shootings.

2

EDUCATION

When I bought my first rental property in 1986, a three unit in the northeast section of Reading, I observed the typical working family. Every neighbor up and down that street was employed mostly in manufacturing working the hours of 7:00am to 3:00pm. That meant leaving for work at 6:30am and returning every day at 3:30pm. Their daily routine was based around those work hours. Upon returning from work, they would sweep their front porch and sidewalk and pick up trash that had blown into their backyard during the day saving the city the expense of a street cleaning program. As their children returned home from school, they were there to monitor the afternoon activities of the children such as doing their homework while they prepared dinner. After dinner children were cleaned up and went to bed before 9:00pm.

This routine changed in the early 1990's as the country moved into a deep recession. Many of the citizens of the city faced layoffs as changes came to the industries where they worked. Manufacturing jobs were the best paying jobs so finding another job at the same pay rate was almost impossible since those jobs were all leaving the area. Some took another job at a greatly reduced pay rate while others sat on unemployment until it ran out and then went looking for another job. With different jobs also came different work hours mostly 8:30am to 5:00pm. The children who were old enough to stay by themselves came home to an empty, unsupervised home. They did not sit down and do homework but instead went out to play or brought friends home. Getting out of school at 3:00pm meant that they had two and a half hours of no supervision and no influence of a parent. By the time the parent arrived home, there was no time for cleaning up the sidewalk in front of their home or cleaning up the backyard. The parent was busy making dinner and by the time dinner was over, everyone was too tired to think about homework so assignments were done either haphazardly or not at all. Many inner-city school districts stopped assigning homework. Many children went to school without breakfast and teachers found it impossible to teach hungry children. City schools offered children breakfast before school started. Not only were children not getting breakfast at home, but were not given a packed lunch or money to buy lunch. The free or reduced lunch program was introduced to solve that problem. From knowing them very well I can honestly say that for many, this was more of a parent being overwhelmed than a monetary problem.

In 1992 I bought a four unit next to the three unit I already owned. I was then managing seven units in that location. The high school was up the street and when students were dismissed in the afternoon, the police sat in squad cars on every block because of the vandalism that occurred while they walked home. The students picked up recycling cans and threw them at cars driving down the street. At least once a week a fight broke out on street corners between students. As a result, many families moved out of the city to the new construction homes being built in the surrounding suburbs. Families broke up resulting in a high rate of families headed by single parents. Homes were converted into apartment buildings housing multiple families living in close quarters leaving inadequate parking. Property taxes rose so that they were the highest in the county which was another incentive for people to move. Although the Reading School District was boasting that they had the best facilities in the county, they also had the largest drop-out rate, the largest incidence of teenage pregnancy, and the lowest test scores. In an attempt to remedy their problems, they were emphatic about having state of the art facilities and the best qualified teachers. They were seeking teachers with advanced degrees and were paying some top salaries. We saw all of this money spent without any positive change in the students.

To pay for all of this state of the art takes a lot of money. In answer to that I saw steady tax increases on all property I owned inside of the city limits. In addition to that a business privilege tax was added and transfer tax was increased to 2.5% instead of the 1% that was everywhere else in the county. Property values steadily dropped. When the city was no longer able to raise taxes, they raised water and sewer rates. Many property owners as well as businesses moved out leaving the city with a greatly diminished tax base. The city must continue to cut expenses when this occurs. City wide trash collection was eliminated leaving residents responsible for hiring their own private trash collection at their own expense. In further cost cutting. The police force was reduced drawing criminals from out of the area who are always looking for places where crime pays.

In the mid 1990's as a real estate agent at a local company, we attended a once a week meeting mainly to tour new listings. For every occupied home in the city we toured, we toured ten vacant homes. Just several years earlier when I was first licensed, for every vacant home we toured there were ten occupied homes. Since the market was flooded with city homes, many of those homeowners chose not to rent them, but kept them vacant until they were sold. Many had lived in the city long enough to pay off their mortgages and save another down payment for a new home outside the city. Because of the surplus of inventory, it was not uncommon to see a home in the city sit on the market for a couple of years. Many vacant homes in the city were winterized and the water turned off at the curb at the request of the homeowner. That meant that the city was really not benefiting from the hike in water and sewer rates that they anticipated or needed.

This was at the point where I saw a major shift occur in the city. No one wanted to live there and the people who did, had no choice. They could rent an apartment cheaper there than anywhere in the suburbs. Many of my tenants went from steady people with jobs, to people always in between jobs. With the loss of manufacturing jobs, those employees could not think of buying a home and therefore were long term renters. I began to see rent collection problems. For six years I rented to people who stayed all of that time to save a down payment for a home in the suburbs. Those people's rent checks arrived in my mailbox before the first of the month and no later than the third. For some who had no checking account I collected theirs in person. There was no reason to have a late payment clause in leases because no one was late.

Many men became unemployable as existing jobs were able to be more selective in choosing the best most qualified worker. This caused a lot of women in the inner city to become the sole support of the family while men remained unemployed for long periods of time and well past the end of collecting unemployment. With limited income, good daycare was unaffordable and the unemployed man in the household became the daycare provider.

There are some men that are excellent daycare providers but those men have made a decision to leave employment to provide daycare and are not men who lost a job so it was easier for them to look after the kids. Instead of being in charge of after school routine with school age children, they were working on cars, hanging out with friends on the corner, or sitting in front of the TV all day. Eventually many of these families broke up leaving a very high percentage of children headed by single parents.

By the time these children reached high school, their parents were fined for truancy on a regular basis. While waiting in district court for my landlord/tenant cases to be called, I listened to many crying mothers that had lost control of their children. Many feared for their children's lives as I heard over and over that their child had become involved in a very dangerous gang. It wasn't uncommon to pick up the newspaper and see that a school age student had been gunned down in an alley. Teenage pregnancy was a common lifestyle and to try to encourage young moms to graduate from high school, daycare was set up inside the school. I watched many young mothers walking home from school pushing a baby in a stroller.

How do all of these problems come out of a school district with state-of-the-art facilities and top teachers? The breakdown of the family unit caused by unemployment was what I observed. Joblessness caused financial pressure in family relationships and eventually family breakdown. Problems such as poverty, unemployment, drug addiction, mental illness, and prison time are examples of what takes parents attention away from their children. Our government has attempted to intervene and help children by counseling their parents and offering programs such as head start for very low-income families where this is most likely to occur. Case workers work closely together with families to provide counseling on feeding children nutritious meals involving the four basic food groups as well as other issues relating to children. As much as some help for families is better than no help, the fact that the children spend the majority of time with parents who lead high risk lifestyles leaves only a slim possibility their children will adopt a better lifestyle.

The education system cannot be entirely responsible for the failure of the students. Today teachers are closely monitored and have to be accountable for teaching. Public schools are required to follow guidelines set up by their state and are closely monitored. Private schools work very hard to attract students whose parents are willing to pay tuition because they feel the education is better than the free education that they are entitled to through the public school system. If they are not sent to school ready to learn, no school can be responsible for what happened in this child's life for the first five years before entering school, a foundation that largely determines success or failure in life. In the many units I walked through over the years, I witnessed the seeds of failure planted all the way back as early as infancy. Many are behind in school and are later diagnosed with learning disabilities. No matter how much early intervention they have, they are never caught up.

Alongside of these failing students in the same classrooms are students that are performing extraordinarily well, graduating at the top of their high school classes and going on to be accepted at some top universities. They are then graduating from those fine universities to be immediately offered top jobs and going on from there to live very productive and rewarding lives.

A TALE OF TWO FAMILIES

Pablo

I had two large apartments side by side that housed mostly families who usually stayed ten plus years. The location was close to both the elementary and high school making it very convenient for students to walk to both schools. A Mexican family, husband, wife and a daughter aged ten and a son, age eight applied for the apartment. The parents spoke no English, their son being the translator for them. Both children were very fluent in English and Spanish, but through the ten years that they lived there, all my conversations were mostly with Pablo. Both parents worked in mushroom farming and left very early to catch the bus for work. Both children got ready by themselves and walked together to school. In the afternoon, the parents arrived home from work at 3:30pm and the children at 3:40pm. Upon arriving home, the mother cooked a hot meal usually in a large pot on the stove. The children sat in the living room with their father where they had small desks from a second-hand shop and completed their homework. After dinner, the mother cleaned up the kitchen and packed everyone's lunch for the next day.

I saw this routine during rent collections or maintenance visits. In ten years, never once were they late in paying rent. Both had steady work the entire time they rented the apartment never missing one day of work. They had no TV, no car, no frills, just the basic necessities. They did not collect food stamps or any government subsidies and their children were not on the free lunch program.

One afternoon as I entered the living room to collect the rent, Pablo sat next to his father reading a book in English. His father had no clue what his son was reading but he was pointing to a picture of a dog on the page and laughing. This was part of the reading program offering coupons for Pizza Hut if a student read books aloud to parents and the parent signed forms verifying that the student had actually read the books.

Eventually the daughter graduated from high school and went off to college on a scholarship. Several years later Pablo graduated at the top of his high school class and was accepted on a full scholarship to Columbia University. Pablo, in complying with the terms of the lease gave a thirty-day notice that his parents would be moving. Since he was moving away to go to college his parents would be moving from the apartment to live closer to relatives who could help them with what Pablo always helped them with.

Jessica

I rented the apartment next door to Pablo's family during the same time period to a family consisting of a mother, father and a daughter, nine years old, all born and raised in this country. It was the parent's second marriage both having grown children living on their own from prior marriages. When I asked why they were moving from their prior apartment in the suburbs, they told me it was too expensive. It was obvious upon reviewing their application why they couldn't afford their previous apartment and I really questioned whether or not they could afford my apartment. The mother worked at a job paying minimum wage and the father was unemployed but I was assured that he was in the process of being hired to work for the state. I rented the apartment to the family and the rent was a problem from the beginning. They were always short with the promise of the balance being paid in two weeks when she would be paid again. There was always an excuse such as their car broke down, their cat needed to go to the vet, or there was an unexpected medical emergency. She always assured me that this was only temporary because her husband would be returning to work within the next thirty days.

For the next five years her husband remained unemployed. While she was at work and the daughter at school, he sat in the apartment chain smoking and watching old black and white movies. Meals consisted of take out, mostly picking up a pizza. Stacks of empty pizza boxes were always piled up on top of the refrigerator until someone put them in the trash. I never saw any meal being prepared on a stove but mostly prepackaged meals or snacks that require no more effort than heating up in an oven or microwave. The kitchen table was piled high with mail, some unopened and other junk making it impossible to eat at. I never saw this family interacting with each other spending most of their time separated in rooms.

When the daughter was about fourteen years old, the husband found a job. Neither parent returned home from work until 5:30pm. A few months later on a maintenance check, I saw Jessica come home with a boy and enter the apartment at 3:30pm. I knew how this story would end. They had a few hours a day alone in the apartment and it didn't take long before Jessica became pregnant at the age of fourteen. With her father working full time her parent's finances were no better than they were before as they continued to be late with their rent. They fell far enough behind forcing me to file for eviction. They left in the middle of the night moving into a motel that rents by the week. Jessica dropped out of high school and had the baby which caused her to be dependent on government programs for financial support.

Comparison of Families

In analyzing these two families, there are drastic differences inside the family dynamics. Pablo had two exceptional parents who both work not only outside the home but inside as well. Their workday ends before their children get home from school so that they never come home to an empty house. They live on what they earn which is why they are able to pay all their bills on time with no stress. Their money was never spent on items such as vehicles or pets that require unexpected maintenance which is very difficult on a low income. They ate healthy home cooked meals and got plenty of rest to be able to perform well at both work and school.

No one ever got sick enough to see a doctor which eliminates health care expense. Even though the parents' incomes were very low, they made it work on what they earned. They were not dependent on the government or anyone to subsidize childcare, food stamps, or any other program that the tax payers pay for.

Looking at Jessica's family we have one adult supporting two adults, a child, a pet, a car, TV cable, take-out meals, prepared foods and impulsive spending on minimum wage. There was a great difference in energy levels between Pablo and Jessica's parents. This may have something to do with smoking and prepared foods lacking in nutrition affecting their child who looked underweight and pale most of the time. In looking at the contrast further, Jessica's mother has all of the adult responsibility piled on her and is safe to say that she is more of a single parent with a grown child and a child. Jessica will not grow up with the same benefits as Pablo who has good role models.

I saw very few children like Pablo and many more like Jessica come and go over years of property management. Inner city education systems struggle to be parents to children by filling the voids that they experience at home such as not being served regular meals or the need for childcare for infants born to the students. Students having children in high school put those mothers at risk for a life of dependency on government assistance for support. In an attempt to raise them up from this type of life there are many college scholarships available to them and they are encouraged to take advantage of them. As a society we are motivated to offer free education in hopes that we can lift people out of poverty to function productively and contribute in a positive way. If this were to happen with every person that we help, we could be a great society, however, we rarely see that result.

Other School Options

Many parents were caught in their first home in the inner city that was supposed to give them that start towards a better life in the suburbs. They were stuck there after manufacturing jobs left causing falling real estate values, increased property taxes, and unemployment they may have faced. This meant they were unable to afford to move and unable to afford private school. With the increasing social problems in the Reading School District, many expressed concerns about their children falling into the wrong crowd resulting in having lasting effects on their future lives. Having no other options, home schooling became popular.

While viewing investment property, I walked into a home school situation that I was immediately very impressed with. It was a two-unit apartment building with the first floor set up as a school room with five middle and high school students sitting at desks all working individually with a mother of one of the students supervising. Walking by the students, I noticed that they were all working on advanced curriculums. The oldest boy, a senior, had already had several college acceptances. A group of parents had gotten together on the block and decided that they were going to home school their children because of the social problems in the Reading School District. All of the parents were involved in the schooling and each parent taught all of the children a certain subject. Several mothers were home during the day to teach subjects and the fathers taught at night after returning from their daytime jobs.

There was another advantage of home schooling, the curriculum can be customized for each student as what I had observed in this small home school setting. Instead of lecturing to a group of students, I observed a parent monitoring while each student followed an individual study program in a book customized for them. Since the group is small and the parent is on top of the group, it is very unlikely that any student falls behind or just stops working. If he gets stuck or has a question, the parent is immediately available to help. Another advantage is that parents can control what their child is taught. There are too many subjects taught in public schools that are not beneficial to students and many of value that have been dropped from curriculums.

Advance Education in Inner Cities

I signed many forms for tenants verifying their address so that they could receive grant and scholarship money for college. This is not to be mistaken for academic or sports scholarships that were earned by the students who receive them for the hard efforts and much extra time that they have spent above and beyond the average. These are scholarships that are need based solely on income. Free education for many was considered to be a way to support one's self instead of what it was designed to do. The fact that many of these programs came with housing vouchers, utility allowances and food stamps was enough of an incentive to get into the program versus getting a college degree to better yourself.

There are many basics of life that need to be mastered before any program would ever lift people up and out of poverty. A college degree will not make a person a better person if they don't have good values to begin with. Going to college just to be supported by the government is not working hard to become skilled and will not result in job opportunities that they think they are entitled to after graduation. Instead, many would be better off getting a job and working hard to master skill to become valuable enough to advance. Much of what is learned over a person's lifetime is on the job rather than what is learned in the short time they spend in school. School will teach you the basic fundamentals and most of what you learn in school you will never use on the job.

At the time that I signed many address verifications mostly between 2009-2015, for students to be able to continue to get free money for education, they would have to maintain at least a C- average. A C- average is not by any means exceptional. If they were able to achieve that some were unable to complete a degree in four years. This may have been a lack of motivation due to the fact that as soon as they did their benefits would stop. A person having this lack of motivation always seemed to have trouble finding a job in their field. Most do find jobs that they did not need college for at all. Many of the recipients do not have a good prior academic track record resulting in dropping out of high school. This means that they have finished high school online with a general equivalency program (GED). Most that I housed never finished college but if they did, they generally stayed in the same type of job that they had before entering college.

We can't blame the college that they attended or the teachers that they had. I knew many people through home sales that graduated from those same colleges with those same majors who worked at jobs at a much higher salary, none of them having collected government subsidies. They were able to save money, buy homes in nice neighborhoods and have a great quality of life.

Many of those that I housed with a general equivalency diploma struggled in life and with employment. They missed the high school experience of interacting socially and being a part of sports programs or other programs offered where the opportunity of finding a lifelong passion may exist. They also miss out on competition and an awareness of where they stack up in relation to others. I am not saying that you should be competing with others, but you should be aware of your limitations. It makes no sense and is a complete waste of time to pursue a career where you will fall below average in comparison to others. This means problems with finding employment or working at a below average salary in that field.

Jeremy

I rented an apartment to an unmarried couple with two children and living on welfare. Jeremy, the father was attending an excellent college free full time. He also worked at a nearby convenience store, a job that he could walk to.

When he finished college with a business degree, the convenience store offered him the manager's job which he turned down. The store was located in a high crime neighborhood so their selection of applicants for that job were very limited which made this such a good opportunity for him. If he applied for this job anywhere else, I don't believe he would have had a chance due to the tougher competition to work in a more desirable area. When I asked him why he turned down the job, he decided it wasn't worth the added responsibility. He was expecting more of an increase after getting his college degree in business so instead he stayed at his present job as a cashier. He was unable to see that the manager's job was a stepping stone to a district managers job and many more opportunities.

When we start with students who have exceptional qualities, we are bound to have successful results. One of our education goals for this country should be to identify those really top, very hardworking students, as they are the ones that will contribute great things to our society such as finding cures for diseases and inventions that will change our lives profoundly.

3

OUR FAILING SCHOOLS

A teacher with twenty years of teaching experience was investigated after a group of parents filed complaints against her because half of her class was failing. These failing students were tested by the school psychologist for learning disabilities and determined not to be learning disabled. The parents concluded that the school psychologist was incompetent and were retested by an outside psychologist with the same result. The parents then concluded that the teacher was incompetent. The superintendent required the principal to constantly monitor this teacher by regularly observing her teaching in the classroom to find nothing out of the ordinary. Not only is this a distraction to the class but it forces the principal to work extra hours to complete the work she is not doing while observing the class.

There is extra tutoring help available in public school systems funded by the state for those who qualify determined by testing. None of the children tested low enough to be eligible for that help. Many parents hired their own tutoring services who tutored their children throughout the school year as well as into the summer. By the time these students reached middle school and were still failing no matter how much tutoring they had, the parents were irate.

Studies show that children who are failing in school are at risk for drug abuse, criminal behavior and dropping out in high school. If successful students are social, there is a good chance that failing students can become their friends at an impressionable age. This is why many parents make a different school choice if this should happen in their children's school environment.

When I attended first grade in a lower middle-class school district in the early 1960's we were taught to read in a classroom of thirty-five children with one teacher and no aide. Every child was successful and all were able to read at least on par by the end of December. No one was labeled as "learning disabled" or needing remedial help. This was accomplished by separating students into three groups depending on their ability determined solely by the teacher. The top group, were the "blue birds," the average group were the "red birds," and the low group, the "yellow birds." Most of the students were "red birds" which made sense as most of the population is average. The second largest group, were the "blue birds" or the top group. The smaller group, the "yellow birds" needed a little extra help. The teacher spent more time with the "yellow birds" and had extra assignments for the other groups. If we finished those assignments, we were encouraged to choose a book from her small library to read. By the end of December, the "yellow birds" no longer existed but all flew up to "red bird" status. That is what I would classify as no child left behind.

My children attended two public schools and two private schools from kindergarten through high school.

Since that time, I have researched and read many articles addressing our failing education system in addition to doing volunteer work at all schools my children attended. At every back to school night it was stressed by all teachers that they needed the parent's help in educating their child. Most homework would be assignments with the objective of reviewing what was learned in school that day. We as parents were not to do the assignments or help them but to simply monitor this after school routine to instill this habit that would ensure their success in school for many years to come without parents having to monitor this study hour by the upper grades of elementary school. These assignments would be most valuable if they were completed immediately upon arriving home from school before the dinner or bedtime routine took place. This is exactly how homework was handled when I attended school in the 1960's. I made it a priority to be home every day at 2:30pm when my children got home from school to make sure that this homework routine was completed Monday through Thursday when it was assigned. The other parents whose children were succeeding also made that a priority. They either worked part time in the morning or were self-employed as I was working schedules around children.

With teachers being questioned and blamed for failing students they have no option but to "dumb" their programs down if they want to keep their jobs. With little homework assigned to reinforce learning, it is impossible for most to successfully take a test so there is more focus on projects or group projects (with help from parents) than testing. This is why students test low on national scholastic assessment tests. To fix that problem some schools would spend weeks before the testing teaching the test.

Through volunteer work in my children's schools in the 1990's I couldn't help but notice some drastic developmental lags in students versus the minor ones in the 1960's. To address these developmental lags today, schools have hired extra staffing to meet those needs. That includes more teachers to accommodate smaller classes as well as aides.

Early Education

Our first teachers are our parents or caregivers, whoever we spend the most time with after we are born. Those people have tremendous influence in our lives and are the most important in determining our success in school. They are our one on one teacher who gives us the most individual attention that we will ever have. They are the role models that we learn certain behaviors and lifestyles from. If there are younger children in our family, we observe how those children are cared for and that influences how we will take care of our own children. I remember my mother shopping for food and clothing for us, cleaning the house, gardening, braiding rugs, knitting, sewing, and working outside the home when we were older. My mother spent time teaching us many of the skills that she had even though many we did not pursue in addition to other skills. We learned to write our name, tie our shoes, use scissors, recite the alphabet, sit still and complete tasks all before we entered school. We had toys in a playroom and a swing set and sandbox in the backyard. In other families we observed the same kind of care being given to the children by their parents. Children were sent to preschool several mornings a week to interact and learn socialization skills with other children. In kindergarten in addition to that socialization during playtime, we also sat at desks and worked on work sheets. In first grade we learned to read and do simple math and every grade after that the work became more complicated and difficult but we worked hard and learned a lot.

When we were small children our parents taught us discipline. They set up a schedule for us and we followed it. They expected us to wake up, eat meals, take naps, and go to sleep at night all according to a schedule they set up. We did not decide the schedule because they knew what was best for us. We were taught to have a good attitude, be respectful, and clean up after ourselves. Our parents corrected us when we were wrong or disrespectful without being abusive.

When parents do not set up schedules and routines while teaching their children discipline day in and day out, an enormous burden is placed on our education system as teachers are forced to take a lot of time out to correct students instead of teaching the class. Many are sent to school unprepared to learn and are disrupting others student's education. If teachers try to do any disciplining at all they are reprimanded by their superiors who are fearful of lawsuits from the parents.

It's no wonder that this lack of discipline shows up in test scores today.

Many of the issues I witnessed while doing volunteer work in suburban school districts were the same as what I saw in inner city impoverished school districts. Children born into poverty have caregivers who have problems which distract them from the attention given to their child at the very early education stage. As babies I observed many being left alone in playpens for hours with the TV blasting and little interaction between the child and their caregivers. Much of the individualized attention that happens very early in advantaged children's lives does not happen nearly as much in children who grow up in problematic homes. Therefore, those children are the first to experience developmental lags and easily fall behind.

Parents do not spend the time with their children as they once did in the early education stage. Their children may go to daycare where the caregiver's attention is shared by other children. There are other parents, mostly moms, who stay home full time but still don't spend the time with children as they once did. Today there are far more distractions such as shopping, appointments, many errands, to name a few that they are involved in instead of activities with their children. If they were to keep time sheets of just where their time is spent, this could be an eye opener. There is a growing number of people with mental illness such as depression that is no longer just an inner-city problem. Many people who suffer from depression are not able to interact with their children having no option but to leave them in playpens for hours. When those children start school there is a very drastic difference between them and the children who came from an early education setting with attentive parents.

Unlike the youth from the inner-city, the youth from the suburbs come from families who have money to hire extra tutoring help. This is what keeps these suburban students in school and graduating. Tutoring businesses seemed to spring up everywhere around the year 2000 and included SAT tutoring to elevate those scores with money back guarantees. With that came another business of college counseling. Some of those counselors had worked as guidance counselors in schools and some had no more experience than getting college admission at top schools for their own children. Recently we have become aware of a counselor actually falsifying test scores and other information to gain students admissions to schools they don't begin to qualify to be admitted to. This not only takes spots from students who do qualify but more importantly it places students who don't qualify in positions where it is very difficult for them to succeed setting them up for lifelong failure.

4

EMPLOYMENT

A country's greatest resource is employment because if there is no employment that country has nothing to offer but poverty. America has always been known as the land of opportunity and the place to work and provide a better life for families. Our ancestors came to America with this goal in mind and were beyond grateful to find a place like our country where hard work would be greatly rewarded making dreams come true for them. Many came to America leaving a life of poverty behind in the country where they were born with no guarantees but were willing to take that risk for the promise of a much better life. When our ancestors arrived, they were willing to do any job just so long as they had one. Welfare, food stamps, housing allowances, housing contents allowances or any other entitlement programs did not exist. America was built on the hard work of those who came to this country and made it great.

Today there are a lot of great employment opportunities and more plentiful than when our ancestors first came to this country. They provide comfortable work environments with heat and air conditioning which did not exist previously. Also, unlike the past there are labor laws preventing businesses from operating as sweat shops. Somehow, our ancestors were always able to find their way in a country that offered them far less, while today we have many who are unemployed and rely on some form of government assistance.

When I was growing up, I didn't know one person who was unemployed. I don't remember companies moving or going out of business. There was a job that everyone could do and everyone liked what they did. Today is different as many jobs have been sent out of the country when our citizens could very well do those jobs and succeed at them. Since those jobs are unavailable, they don't feel they have a choice but to go to college. This has created a much larger demand for college causing college tuition to soar. Many college graduates are unable to find a job because of job scarcity in relationship to what it had been many years ago. They are forced into jobs that they are not good at or they have no real passion for. This only leads to failure and unemployment. Many people go through cycles of quitting jobs or being fired for below average performance. This happens at all different levels including minimum wage jobs up to some high level high paying jobs. I showed a man an apartment who sounded great on the phone. He was equally great in person except for one thing. He was employed at a fast-food restaurant part time. I asked him why he was working just part time and he said, "it's almost impossible to find full time employment in this day and age." This was during a time when the economy was good with help wanted signs in many windows of businesses. I did not rent the apartment to him because I didn't believe he could afford it working just part time. Several months later I happened to stop into the fast-food restaurant where he was working to pick up take out. He was behind the counter struggling to keep orders straight while he burned the fries and spilled coffee. He had a difficult time multi-tasking and would have probably been better suited to a job in manufacturing which is more repetitive in nature. At that time those jobs had left Reading forcing people like this guy into jobs they are not proficient at.

Amanda

I listed a condo for sale for a young woman who had been out of college for seven years. When she graduated from a good college with very good grades, she was unable to find a job in the major she pursued. Worse yet she was unable to find a job for any amount of what she felt was a respectable salary. Feeling defeated she took a job that she could have had right out of high school and decided she would keep looking. Much to her surprise she really liked the job and did extremely well. The company was looking for talent like her and she was promoted many times within the company. I was selling her condo and she was moving out of state for another very big promotion with that same company.

Some people don't make the right choice as Amanda did which was taking some job instead of waiting for that job to come to them. If you are really good at that job you will get promoted or you will gain the necessary skills that you need to go to a better job. When people decide to do nothing, they miss those opportunities and time passes.

Lifting People Up

As we search for solutions to lift low income people out of poverty, we have a tendency to put laws in place regarding minority quotas and requiring businesses to have a specific percentage of employees who fall under those minority classifications. This practice forces companies to promote or hire people who fall below the standard that job requires for the sole reason to be in compliance. It is never good to put people in jobs they are not able to do. This only holds a person back further and causes minorities who are really good at what they do to become resentful knowing that they were not hired for their skill but only to fill a quota.

January 1977

On my first day of a new job a black female, Janis, was assigned to train me. It was obvious to me that was the last thing Janis wanted to do but she was leaving the company and I was hired to fill her place. She was angry and resentful and my training was unpleasant to say the least. I got the feeling that Janis was leaving for personality conflicts, it certainly had nothing to do with her ability to do the job. She was very smart, quick and could keep many details in her head and recall them in an instant never having to look up anything. Her attitude made me uncomfortable and I was relieved when she went to lunch one day and never came back. Before that happened though, between her sarcastic remarks regarding the company, I realized why she was so resentful. In the middle of my training one day I remarked to Janis that she seemed quite angry about something and I was starting to become worried about the culture of this company.

"Don't worry" she said, "you will fit in just fine because you are white"

"what do you mean" I asked.

"It's just what I said, they don't want me here at all, look around you, I'm the only black person here in a sea of white faces"

"Why would you say that, it appears to me that you are really good at your job, I can definitely see why you would be hired, you were probably a top applicant for this job"

"wow, are you naïve, I was the only candidate"

"I'm not sure that I understand what you mean"

"I mean you are clueless to think that I was hired for my skill. That is what I should have been hired for but I was obviously hired to fill some minority quota and that's why I'm leaving. I am not going to spend my time helping a bunch of white racists fill some quota. If it weren't for that quota, I would never have been hired in the first place. They can take their quota and shove it."

Little did I know at the time that I would leave this company one year later over minority quotas. After Janis left, they were back to looking to fill their minority quota again. This can be a real problem if no one with the needed skills applies for the job which is what happened. This leaves a company to go looking for someone who will work for them. They found a black female that was presently working somewhere else so they had to make their offer very attractive for her to leave that job. Denise was exempt from the usual practice of screening and testing to make sure that she was a good fit for the job. It turned out that the job she was hired to do, she was unable to do. I was assigned a lot more additional responsibility in addition to being assigned all of the tasks that she was required to do while she sat at her desk and did very little.

This became stressful and gave me no alternative but to look for another job. When I gave my boss notice that I was leaving, he was shocked. He asked me why and I told him it was the added responsibility of Denise's work. My boss told me that I should be a little more understanding about Denise. He went on to say that the reason she was unable to do her job was that she was from a poor urban neighborhood and I'm luckier than she is because I have had advantages growing up that she has not. Therefore, we need to give her a chance and everyone needs to chip in and help her out. I told him that I didn't mind helping but piling all of her work on me only left me feeling very stressed out and taken advantage of. Not surprising was the fact that they hired three people to do my job after I left.

Minority quotas leave everyone in disadvantaged situations including those that they are trying to help. They kill all motivation for people they are trying to serve of ever striving to be their best since they don't have to compete by constantly finding ways to better themselves. It left both Janis feeling resentful and Denise feeling helpless which will eventually undermine their sense of self-worth.

In the 1970's when I was first exposed to minority quotas, many businesses considered women to fall into a minority class. No one should be rewarded for the sole reason that they are a woman. When I hear women say things like, "I believe more woman should be promoted" or "I am interested to know how many women are in top positions in a certain field or within a certain company" it has alerted me to the fact that these women desperately need that edge and they are probably not the best candidate.

As a business owner, I searched for the very best to work for me or serve me. I certainly did not want to come from a mindset of charity and give someone a job because they fell below my standards and were looking for me to be charitable. When the people we hire are not a good fit it hurts the business and causes the best people to leave. No business can afford to stay in business long term when they don't have every employee working at their maximum potential.

February 1992

I rented an apartment to Jasmine and her boyfriend Andre. They looked barely old enough to sign a lease but assured me that she was eighteen and he twenty-one. As young as Jasmine looked, I felt better about her than I did about Andre. Jasmine was a waitress at a nearby steakhouse and Andre was looking for a job. Jasmine never missed a day of work while Andre kept losing jobs that he was hired to do. He always had a lot of excuses as to why he had trouble with employment but I could always depend on Jasmine to pay the rent. About six months into the lease, Jasmine became pregnant. She waitressed all the way up until the day that she went into premature labor at which time she had a cesarean section keeping her off of work for six weeks. Her eighty-year old grandmother came every day to help her with the baby while Andre either hung out with friends on the corner or played video games. One day when I stopped by to collect rent, I found Andre sitting at the kitchen table drawing pictures and smoking marijuana. I sat across the table from him with my receipt book in front of me.

"don't bust my ass about the rent, I don't have it"

"and you won't have it until you go to work, I mean she certainly isn't going back anytime soon, and keep smoking that and you won't pass a drug test to get a job to support your family"

"I don't want a job I want to go to art school"

"It's too late for that, you have a family to support and that requires you to take any job you can get"

I had to file for eviction since they were unable to pay the rent. They left the apartment leaving no forwarding address.

May 2002

Over the years, I have showed up on many people's credit reports as being owed back rent after getting a judgment for an eviction. I hear from few who have the intention of paying me what they owe me but if they do, they have gone on to an improved life. If they are buying a home, it means that they have made major improvements in themselves to be able to get steady employment that will pay them enough to save for a home. During the mortgage application process, they are encouraged by their loan officer to call those on their credit report and try to negotiate those loans off.

I was somewhat surprised to receive an email from Jasmine regarding the $800 in back rent that she owed me from ten years previously. The email said that she was trying to buy a home to make a better life for herself and her ten-year old special needs daughter and that she would appreciate it if I would completely forgive the loan since the lease was not valid anyway due to the fact that she was only sixteen at the time. I wrote her back and said that I would not. She wrote me back again and asked if I would accept half of the money for her share of the back rent. I wrote back and told her again that I would not. She had signed a joint lease with Andre and they collectively owed $800. I didn't care who paid it but would not release the lien until it was paid in full. I certainly did not need the $800 after ten years and it really didn't matter to me whether they paid it or not.

A year later I thought of Jasmine one day and wondered if she ever bought a house. I could have easily run a public records search but was busy with other real estate business. Just as I was wondering, I received another email from her asking why I never cashed the check. I asked her what check she was referring to as I had never received a check. She asked if she could call me. She explained that she had bought a house a year ago and the title company was going to send me a check for the $800 that they had collected at settlement. She expected that I would remove the lien after I received the check however, not only did I not receive it I didn't know about it. After a few phone calls, Jasmine found out that it was lying at the bottom of a pile on a title clerk's desk. She asked if I would meet her at the courthouse and sign off on the lien if she gave me the money in the form of a treasurer's check.

As I walked off the elevator, I saw Jasmine standing at the double doors of the prothonotary's office.

"You still look the same," she said

"you too, I said.

We walked through the doors and explained to the clerk behind the counter what we were there for. She handed me the check and I released her lien. We walked back out in the hallway and I asked her what happened in her life over the last ten years. She had gone to college and had gotten a business degree while working full time and raising her daughter who challenged with multiple learning disabilities. I asked her if Andre had been involved in the raising of their daughter and she said that he had not. She then added that she never received one dime of child support from him. She had been the sole provider for her daughter with no help from anyone. Her grandmother who had raised her had died shortly after her daughter was born.

When it was time to leave, I hugged her and said, "congratulations, you will do good things with the rest of your life." She looked puzzled and I explained to her that only the best rise above and out of poverty and the exceptional do it alone.

A year later I saw her wedding announcement in the paper. Both she and her husband had college degrees, good jobs, and were living in the suburbs. Jasmine had grown up in one of the poorest most crime ridden neighborhoods in Reading. I knew that she would one day rise above it and find success in her life in spite of her disadvantaged background. I knew this because of her great positive attitude, her pleasant personality, her beautiful smile, her hard work ethic and her determined nature.

If we want to be successful in life, we all have to take steps by ourselves to be successful. No one can give us success it has to be earned as Jasmine earned it. We can't make people be successful or want to be successful no matter how much money or opportunity we give to them. I told my children all of the time, "you need to make it happen for yourselves, I wish so much that I could do that for you but I can't." This is true of everyone. We give thousands of dollars through government programs to help people rise up and out of poverty but until they decide to do it by themselves, it won't ever happen.

5

IMMIGRATION

Many businesses are in desperate need of hardworking employees causing them to turn to other countries to tap into their human resources. A country like Mexico has little employment opportunity in comparison to the United States so Mexicans are more than happy to leave their country for better opportunities. Every day that an employer doesn't fill a position, is money lost to that business. Over anxious to fill these positions, some employers will skip the proper vetting process. In more recent years, most do require proper identification which can be bought illegally almost anywhere.

It was well known that many illegal people mainly from Mexico were living in Reading as far back as I remember when I moved to Reading in 1979. They commonly came to Reading to work in mushroom farming, a job that our citizens wanted no part of. Americans have to be willing to take the jobs that are available instead of saying that they do not want to do that kind of work to prevent jobs from being taken by people living in this country illegally.

For many years I read the local paper every day from the first day that I moved to Reading. In the early 1980's a woman's dead body was found wrapped in an old carpet and dumped in brush near the mushroom houses. The woman had never been identified or reported as missing but it was determined that she was a woman of Mexican descent in her mid-twenties. That was the only article that appeared about that murder in the paper. Investigators believed that she was in the country illegally most likely murdered by another person in this country illegally. That would make this murder very difficult to solve no matter how much effort was put into it. It was not a concern for our citizens at the time as it did not involve any of them. Slowly over a period of time that changed.

During the 1980's a number of rapes occurred near the mushroom houses, the victims being our own citizens. This information appeared in the back pages of our local newspaper that many were not aware of because they either didn't read the paper regularly or they stopped reading after the first few pages. The victims were pulled into wooded areas at knifepoint while jogging, and raped but not beaten or killed. They were able to provide a description to a composite artist and a composite sketch would be published in the local paper but always reported with a very small article. The sketches over the years as well as the descriptions in the articles were of different men but all were of Mexican descent. Giving little publicity to these crimes kept our citizens in the dark. They were unaware that any crime like that was occurring and due to the lack of awareness it became more common to see these sexual assaults increase. The word eventually got out and it became common knowledge that anywhere near the mushroom houses was unsafe. Real estate values dropped in that area and as bad as the smell was, the assaults against women were worse.

While vacationing with several other couples in the Caribbean, one of the women in our group talked about her father's extensive travels for business in Mexico. According to her father, it was very common to see a carload of men pull up to a woman walking and rape her one by one while people were driving and walking by. As horrifying as this is to Americans where there are laws in this country that are enforced to protect women, it is common in other countries where those laws either don't exist or are not enforced. This sounded very familiar to what was happening near the mushroom houses.

A police detective told me that they would question nearby mushroom house workers but no one ever recognized the composite sketch. He said the perpetrators were always illegal and as soon as the sketch hit the local paper, they were most likely long gone leaving the country as easily and quickly as they came in.

Then the unthinkable happened. This crime occurred in a neighborhood at the bottom of the hill from a group of mushroom houses. A wooded area separated the mushroom houses from desirable suburban neighborhoods. The forty-year old homes housed original homeowners and only became available for sale privately through the heirs as the owners passed away. A young couple with three small children had moved into one of the homes feeling lucky to raise their family in such a desirable neighborhood. The mushroom houses being hidden by the woods that lined up to their backyard were easy to forget.

One evening, the husband took the kids out to a nearby attraction. The wife, not feeling well, stayed behind to take a bath and go to bed early. When the husband arrived home a few hours later with the kids, he found his wife in the bathtub with her throat slashed. She had bled to death before drowning. The detectives who investigated her death immediately found her husband to be a person of interest. They found the wife's time of death to be very close to the time that he said he left the home with the kids. It was surmised at one point that the husband put the kids in the car before going back into the house and slashing his wife's throat. He then took the kids to a nearby attraction and dinner for two hours in order to have an alibi. There had never been any history of domestic problems and those who knew the couple personally never believed that this could be a possibility. The investigative team had their suspicions since there was no sign of forced entry and nothing appeared to be out of place. Many hours had been spent on this case over several years that never produced any other suspects.

Initially, a neighborhood canvass was done and everyone interviewed claimed that they never saw anything except the husband leave with the kids, which is how the time he left was determined. Not having any other leads or suspects, they did another neighborhood canvass several years later just in case they may have missed something. A woman in her late eighties, who spent her day sitting at her window said that she had been thinking about something she saw several weeks before her neighbor was killed. She had seen a Mexican man standing at the edge of the woods next door. During that time, the neighbor was having remodeling work done to their home and she assumed that he was one of the workers however it was confirmed that no one with that description was ever employed by the remodeling company. Many of the rape victims over the years had told police that they were forced at knife point into the woods. The police came up with a theory that maybe the perpetrator was hiding in the woods behind the house and saw the husband leave without the wife. If he had been watching the house, he would have known exactly who lived there. No one could remember whether or not the back door was locked but if it was left unlocked that would have explained the unforced entry. It took him by surprise when the woman he intended to rape was in the bathtub and instead, slashed her throat and left. The neighbor could not remember what the man in the woods had looked like so police were unable to get a composite sketch and the investigation went no further.

As years went on and more people from Mexico immigrated illegally to this country, it became more common to find the illegal workers to be sitting on curbs and walking around neighborhoods near the mushroom houses. Even though there is no law against this, for neighbors who had lived in these neighborhoods for many years and sometimes for generations, found this undesirable. It was not that they were illegal or of Mexican descent or that the neighbors were prejudice or racist, but it was the threat of the number of rapes that had occurred and had never been brought to justice.

During this time, I listed a home for sale in that area and as I got out of my car to show the home to prospective buyers, there were mushroom workers just hanging around. They looked at us lewdly as we got out of the car and yelled out in Spanish suggestive or inappropriate things. In this nice suburban neighborhood, it became unsafe to walk up and down the street, especially for teenage girls without an adult with them. This is what caused residents to move out in record numbers. The home I listed for sale was beautiful and very well cared for. The sellers were extremely disappointed in the final sales price but the price had everything to do with the location and nothing to do with the condition of their home.

It seemed that most prospective buyers came to view the home after 3:00pm, which was the worst time. That was the time that most mushroom farm workers got off of work and hung around the neighborhood. Often prospective buyers may have an objection to the home but then after seeing more in their price range would go back to considering something that they had initially rejected. In all of the years that I have sold real estate, not one ever came back and considered a home with a neighborhood problem. In this case the feedback from other realtors was always the same. The prospective buyer felt intimidated by the looks from the men sitting on the curbs as they got out of their cars. Furthermore, they assumed that these men sitting on the curbs may be neighbors and felt more threatened.

Whether they were neighbors or not did not matter. What mattered to the prospective buyers is the feeling they got the minute they got out of their car.

April 1994

The house was a fairly easy renovation, a flip that I bought after a Tuesday morning office real estate tour. It was vacant, a total wreck and smelling very badly but I knew the seller needed to unload it. They had lived there long enough to pay the mortgage off and save enough money to buy a new construction home in the suburbs. Home repairs and maintenance were obviously never a priority for these homeowners. I offered them the fairest price I could have figuring that the detached garage in the back added value.

After doing cosmetics only, it was ready for the spring market. One Sunday, I did an open house and only one couple visited that day and eventually bought the house. I sensed something very unusual about this couple. He was a very handsome, well-dressed man of middle eastern descent and she was a very overweight, poorly dressed woman. This couple in about their mid-forties became more unusual the more I got to know them over the next sixty days. During negotiations, we sat at a nearby fast-food restaurant while he made all kinds of demands about what he wanted thrown into the deal for free. I wasn't working with a whole lot of profit margin since the market was on a downturn and getting worse every day, so I didn't want to lose them as buyers.

He had proof of funds from a New York bank to buy three of these homes paying cash for every single one. For someone who was not from the area, he had a very good idea of market values in Reading. He kept asking if he could negotiate directly with the seller and I finally admitted that I was the seller. After the negotiations ended, he dropped out of the picture and I was dealing only with her. She eventually admitted marrying him in exchange for a house fully paid for so that he would be able to gain entry into the United States. Their agreement was that they would have no further contact after the transaction was completed. She claimed that there were entry points into New York where girls stood hoping to make a deal with non-citizens like the deal she had. She told me this was very common and not having an awareness that this existed, it soon became clear to me how it was possible for terrorists to gain entry into this country.

Leah 2009-2019

Leah was sixty-seven years old when she first rented a first-floor unit from me until she died ten years later. She had come to America five years previously leaving a family behind in Jamaica for work. She worked two jobs one cleaning a hospital for eight hours and the other a night job cleaning the courthouse for five hours working at these jobs five days a week. She lived on no government programs or government assistance. She spent every Saturday cooking her meals for the week since her work schedule did not permit her extra time during the week.

She was never late paying rent and had everything she could ever want or need in her apartment to give her a comfortable life. She would voice her complaints about the family living in the apartment above her. They had children up until 3:00am on a school night running back and forth making it difficult for her to get proper rest to go to two jobs the next day. They would drop trash out their windows landing on her front porch that she would have to clean up and she was offended by their foul language. Both of us discussed these complaints with the adults living above her numerous times and the problem was never resolved until they moved out.

I found the answer in Leah's apartment as to why some people immigrate to our country and work and live respectfully while others come here and are a problem. There was a letter in a picture frame hanging on the wall from a state senator congratulating her on becoming a citizen. People who go to the time and trouble of citizenship care very much about our country and abiding by our laws.

Six months before she died, she was diagnosed with cancer and dropped one of the jobs but at age seventy-six was still working full time at the other one. One month before she died, she called me to come by and pick up the rent and told me to leave myself in with my key as she was in bed not feeling well. When I got there, she told me that she had retired from her full-time job the week before. She thanked me for everything I did for her over the years that she rented from me and told me this was the last time we would see each other because she doesn't have any time left and expects to die before the end of the month. I asked her if there was anyone that could stay with her and she told me her daughter was coming from Jamaica. She asked me if she could have an extra key for her daughter and I told her that I would get one made and drop it off.

I had a difficult time believing that this woman was dying as she had always been very strong. I didn't know many that had worked two jobs well into their seventies. If I didn't say goodbye and go over and hug her, I believed that she wouldn't die. As I turned to leave, she said,

"god bless, see you in the afterlife."

"no, I will see you in this apartment next month," I said

"please see that the door is locked behind you," she said.

Several weeks later as I pulled up in front of the building, her daughter was standing on the front step talking with a neighbor wearing a hat with an American flag. I slowly got out of the car as our eyes met.

"I have a key for you,"

"Thank you but I won't need it, my mother passed away three days ago and I have her key. She said softly. "I have family coming to help me clean the apartment out."

6

MIGRATION

2006-2016

When people move to an area, they add to the economy when they buy a home, shop in nearby businesses, and fill employment vacancies. They add to the tax base helping to pay for services such as police, fire, and mental health which keep everyone safe. As the population in the city of Reading grew with a large influx of people from out of the area, primarily New York and New Jersey these people did not add to our economy but instead drained it. They were unemployed, homeless and many required mental health services. If they had children, the children required special services in education due to low test scores and most were on the free lunch program.

Many were attracted by the lower cost of real estate in Reading and with loose lending practices had the ability to take equity out of their homes in New York and New Jersey and invest in rental property in another area such as Reading. Many brought their tenants on government assistance with them since they did not have to live anywhere specifically. Not understanding what they were getting into, it didn't take long before they found out that if you were not there in person when the government deposited the tenant's government assistance, they wouldn't pay their rent.

Out of state investors assumed that tenants would mail rents to a post office box in their home state which didn't happen. They had no connections to local contractors to do needed repairs which caused their buildings to rapidly deteriorate and eventually become uninhabitable. It was difficult to get tenants to sweep out in front of the building in which they lived or to pick up trash that was dropped on the property so landlords repeatedly got fined. The city was forced to implement a street cleaning program that ran machinery to clean the streets once a week. If rentals were not well managed and maintained, eventually good tenants moved out and buildings were taken over by homeless drug addicts. Trash and old furniture were left behind in these vacant buildings which would be dumped on neighboring properties as soon as new homeless people moved in. It was common to see units with large numbers of people residing in them generating excessive amounts of trash sitting for weeks eventually being dumped on neighboring properties since there was no citywide trash collection program. The city would then fine the responsible landlord if they didn't remove it at their expense immediately. With water eventually turned off in these vacant buildings, bathtubs were used as toilets where waste piled up and sat stagnate. Eventually it was common to see large rats entering and exiting that building becoming a health hazard to nearby residents.

The city of Reading was unable to go after these absentee landlords. It was impossible to locate them by certified mail in another state as many listed a post office box or no longer resided at the last known address. Many of these buildings did not have a lender, as the loan was attached to their primary residence in New York or New Jersey in the form of a HELLOC. The only chance the city had of taking back those buildings absent of liens were through sheriff sale for unpaid taxes. Until then, the building remained a nuisance to everyone in the neighborhood. If too many existed on a block, no reputable financial institution would finance new sales on that block and they became uninsurable as well. Values of housing decreased from the neglect of out of town owners.

The city tried to get control by sending out census takers. That failed because so many were untruthful about who lived there or did not answer the door at all. Every year the city mailed landlords a form along with their housing permit attempting to get information on the tenants residing in the building. As transient as tenants were, the information was quickly outdated. The city codes department attempted another method of gaining control of the blight that existed in so many apartment buildings by requiring all landlords to register their buildings with the city. The process of registry included a number of forms to be completed by the owner so that they would be able to locate owners if there were problems. The address of the landlord was tied to his driver's license to eliminate post office boxes. If they did not have a driver's license, they would have to produce a valid passport, state or government issued ID. All rental property owners residing twenty-five miles or more from Reading were required to have a property management service. If their rental properties were incorporated, an EIN number would also be required along with supporting documentation of officers of the company. All rental units were required to obtain a business privilege license. One of the forms required was verification from a licensed trash hauler that they were hired to service that particular address. Many hired a trash company just long enough to get that verification but then discontinued service or discontinued paying for it. They would then return to their old practice of dumping their trash at a neighbor's curb or anywhere else on the property of responsible owners who did pay for trash collection. Trash dumping is considered a quality of life issue carrying a fine for the owner whose property was dumped on.

It was also common to see casual trash dumping such as a young mother stopping to change her baby in a stroller and throwing the dirty diaper on the sidewalk. Children having these bad role models would often throw candy wrappers, soda cans and whatever else as they walked by. I would often see packs of chicken or steak not removed from its wrapper thrown in the street next to the curb. I have no idea why anyone would do this but perhaps they dumped it because it was too heavy to continue to carry home.

A resident residing in a multi-unit next to a multi-unit that I owned dumped a large box that his flat screen TV came in while I sat in my car and watched him do it. I asked him to remove it and he refused. I called the police and he left the property. It took the police two hours to get there and by that time he had come back. He removed the large box when the police told him to remove it only for it to return back on my property several days later.

Registering enabled the city to locate property owners to do regular property maintenance inspections every two years at which time you would be billed for that inspection. If they found violations in the building which most of the time they did because of the abuse by tenants or tenants of neighboring buildings, they would schedule another inspection in sixty days at which time you would be billed again. If all items were not corrected that were listed or were damaged again after they were corrected, the landlord would be fined. If the property owner did not show up for inspections there would also be a fine.

In larger buildings hard wired smoke detectors were required to be installed on every floor and inspected by the fire company. Battery operated smoke detectors were also required inside of all sleeping areas and fire extinguishers in all kitchen areas that were then inspected by the codes department. In my largest building an emergency lighting system was required to be installed in all hallways in case of a fire and that was inspected by building and trades.

The required codes summary were smoke detectors, carbon monoxide detectors, fire extinguishers, peeling paint, a second means of egress, all windows and doors operating correctly, screens in windows, stable flooring with no soft spots, caulk between bathtubs and walls, locksets operating correctly, no sagging ceilings or holes in walls, no broken stair treads, no graffiti, approved trash receptacles, safety and hand rails in place, basement walls in good repair, drip legs on hot water heaters, grounding jumper on water meters, safe electrical wiring. As much as this registration packet was pretty thorough and complete, out of town landlords seemed to find ways around it.

The city codes department was overloaded with complaint calls from responsible owners and more than what could be handled. This forced city government to expand their workforce to meet these incoming calls. This takes more funds to run the city with increased salaries for the additional workers required without increased revenue being brought in.

I found myself most of the time facing stressful situations in my buildings by repeated fines for property violations and damage done to my property by neighboring property owners or their tenants who refused to pay for damage they had caused. The city was owed thousands of dollars by these property owners for violations on their properties that would never be paid while just a few of us paid fines for the damage done to our properties as well as the repair costs.

I owned a building on one end of a block and at the other end was a bar with rooms for rent. In between were a row of five homes operating as illegal rooming houses for many years. Many homes like this were rented to people who were illegally in this country and since the real estate was condemned as far as the city was concerned, they were unoccupied. I brought up the fact that there were mail boxes attached to every house where mail was regularly delivered. The city would come out and knock on the locked doors and no one would answer. Many of these buildings had been condemned for unsanitary and unsafe conditions and of course could not be legally rented until all violations were corrected and they were registered with the city. Because it was not a legal rental, there was no trash collection and for years, their trash was dumped on my property. I repeatedly complained but as long as I couldn't prove it, I was forced to pay for their trash as well as the trash that was generated by all of those homes.

Before the bar at the end of the block went back to the bank, my phone would constantly ring at night with complaints from my tenants. Children were left outside as late as 2:00am cold and crying while their mother sat in the bar. They had called the police but that was an hour ago and they had not responded. I often called child services but they were overloaded with complaints like this all over the city. After the bar went back to the bank, all of the housing did as well. Much of the copper tubing had been ripped out of the buildings and many homeless moved in and lived for months with no running water. Eventually the sewer backed up in the street and when the city entered the building due to the street out front being flooded, they found that sewage had been shoveled in a corner of the basement. Five large sewer rats had come up out of the sewer and were running through the wooden fence between my property and the illegal unit next door. They gained access into my building where one of my tenants killed one by trapping it in a trash can and pouring boiling water over it. Not knowing for sure how many there were altogether, I called in a wildlife expert who baited the basement. Within two weeks the hallway on the first floor smelled heavily of a dead animal. The wildlife expert shoveled four dead rats the size of cats out of the basement. He claimed that he had never seen rats so large and when he brought pictures back to the office of a company that had been in business thirty-five years, they also said they had never seen anything like it. I had been doing rentals in the city thirty years at that point and I had never seen anything like it either. These are conditions that are commonly found in third world countries which breed the worst kinds of infectious diseases. It is against the law for the city to enter a unit without giving a thirty-day notice to whoever is occupying the unit, legally or illegally. If they still can't get access, they have to get a search warrant. This is how conditions with limited law enforcement go on for years.

Eventually these homes were sold to owners from out of state during a very short period of time when the city waived transfer inspections allowing property to be sold in as is condition. The ownership went from absentee owners to people affiliated with out of town street gangs. The city caught up to them to try to enforce codes in homes that were uninhabitable by first requiring them to register. When I filed complaints about the large amounts of trash being dumped on my property the city claimed it was not these residents as they had registered with the name of a legitimate trash hauler. Whenever I went in to city hall to complain that these rental units had no trash pick-up, the city would provide proof on a computer screen that they were legally registered. I could not imagine how any of these homes passed a codes inspection. They also provided proof of a letter from a licensed hauler even though I had not seen regular trash pickup at any of the five residences in question. After they would hire a licensed hauler and never make payment, the hauler would stop trash pickup. Their bags of trash were routinely thrown over my wooden fence separating my property from the one next door or from rooftops into the back area that were once seventeen horse stables that were now dilapidated. These stables were enclosed by a tall chain link fence with a gate and a cement wall bordering along the back of the property. No matter how many times the cement wall was rebuilt it was continually knocked down by vandals.

The codes department ordered me to tear down the horse stables and the Architectural Review Board ordered me to restore them since they were in a historic district. I proposed to put in a parking lot after tear down since parking was at such a premium and was by permit only. The courthouse and many downtown businesses were within walking distance. The parking authority had built a beautiful garage next door which was mostly empty due to the cost to park a car. I was told by the city that they could not approve my parking lot next door because I would be in competition with them. There was no point in spending any money to do this project that would be an enormous improvement for that block when there was no return. Since three city departments could not reach agreements as to what they would permit me to do with the back area there was nothing for me to do but let it continue to deteriorate.

The horse stables became a topic of conversation and were part of a newspaper article. A newspaper reporter called me and asked me if I would agree to be interviewed regarding the matter. I agreed to do a telephone interview in the hopes that it may motivate the three city departments to come up with a reasonable compromise however I would not allow him to take pictures. Pictures of the blight would accomplish nothing but outrageous bids from contractors believing I was being pressured by the city to take action. That happened anyway as contractors began calling me offering their services at prices that were unreasonable.

The codes department loved to bring up these horse stables from time to time and I believe they wanted them torn down, but knew the dilemma all too well. A young new codes officer, unaware of the ten-year battle I had with the city over the horse stables, wrote a violation notice up on the stables ordering me to clean up and remove the debris or be fined. I wanted nothing more than to do this as the area was being accessed from the back of the property and the contents of the five vacant houses were being dumped back there at night. With a violation notice in hand ordering me to clean up was the perfect opportunity to get started. Loads of garbage had been dumped by the illegal rooming houses over the last five years since the last time I had cleaned it up. It began to resemble a land fill as roofs and walls of the stables caved in on the left side. I applied for a dumpster permit and parking permits for five days and brought in a backhoe and a couple of men. Towards the end of the job, Building and Trades came out and shut the job down because I had not applied for a demolition permit. I did not think that was necessary considering I only removed the debris from the deteriorated stables due to vandalism on the left along with 300 bags of trash, mattresses and furniture mixed in with it. The Architectural Review Board was appalled at the fact that the horse stables on the left side were gone without a permit. They required me to come to a meeting with detailed plans of what my intentions were for the right side containing the eight other garages. When I explained at the meeting the problems on that block one of the people on the panel suggested that I should have hung a motion detector lighting system to keep people out of the back at night.

The right side was still in-tact and my original intention was to preserve them converting them into covered parking spaces for small cars. The historic district told me that I would have to install stable doors on them to look original. This creates a problem when this would result in access for the vacant homes to continue to dump trash on my property in concealed areas. After calling a few contractors in for estimates I was told that the structures on the right side were not structurally sound and could present danger to people using them. Their opinions were that they should be completely demolished.

Neighbors had called the police at night when people would start fires in the middle of the stable area. They complained about the possibility of fire spreading making it impossible for them to sleep due to worry. In looking around at the evidence of the fires, it became obvious that they were grilling meat due to the bones left behind. Some of these bones were different than anything I had seen. I then became aware that there were different types of animals that were being raised inside of the illegal rooming houses that were slaughtered and cooked on these makeshift bonfires. Exotic animals were brought into Reading and sold on the black market. In 2017 an unlicensed African Serval female cat was found running around the streets in the city which is illegal to own in Pennsylvania without a license. They sell on the black market for between $20,000 and $30,000. It was presumed that the cat was let out in attempt to breed with a domestic cat which would produce a litter of Savannah cats which are legal to be sold.

The illegal rooming houses had used my stables to deal and shoot drugs, gamble on dog fighting, dump their trash and they also provided shelter for the homeless when the weather was bad. The residents in the illegal rooming houses would walk the dogs on the block with visible injuries such as chunks of fur missing exposing raw skin, and pieces of their ears missing resulting in infections. I called the city repeatedly to report what I had heard from neighbors regarding the dog fighting at night as well as the dog's injuries. All dogs were required to be licensed but as far as the city was concerned, since there was no record of dogs at those addresses that did not exist. When the city would finally get around to investigating the occupants would leave and move into another condemned building to start the process all over again.

At another location regarding dogs the occupants of a third-floor apartment next door would leave their large dogs out on the roof instead of walking them. Since housing was attached in a row, the dogs would wander across the roofs leaving dog dirt all over multiple roofs. The roofs are flat with a slight pitch and when it rained the dog dirt would wash down into the gutters causing water to back up and get under roofs causing thousands of dollars of damage to interior ceilings. I had this repeatedly happen and filed numerous complaints with the city. The owner next door had relatives living in different apartments who did not pay rent so they were not leaving anytime soon. I paid my handyman constantly to shovel off my roof and repair damage to the interior of my adjoining building. The city codes department had so many complaints like this that they couldn't handle them all. When my handyman told the occupants next door to please clean up after their dogs, they threw the dog dirt at my windows. There was no other alternative but to build a fence on the roof to keep the dogs off my roof.

One summer a gang moved into the five vacant homes between my building and the bar. There were six couples and numerous children occupying the houses and operating an illegal car repair on the street. They asked me to open the gate leading back to the horse stables but no one spoke English. One of the women in the group who did speak English ordered me to open the gate as they needed to drop their trash back there and move their car repair shop back there as well.

"No, that is private property," I said. "You cannot have access to work on cars or do anything else back there" I said.

"We have trash that we need to put back there and if I can't get rid of this trash in my house my kid will get sick and I'll sue you." she shouted

"No, in this country it is illegal to dump trash on other people's property, you need to call a trash hauler and pay to have it removed like the rest of us do here in this country." I said

"If you don't open that gate now, I'm gonna kick your fuckin ass" she screamed

"Are you threatening me, because if you are, I'm calling the cops right now," I held up my cell phone.

Of course, that was an empty threat because the police would not come down to this block but these people were new on the block and didn't know that yet. This went on back and forth until one of the guys told the girl to shut up. If things got rough on this block, I could usually depend on one of the drug dealers to step in.

As one of my tenants looked on, he said,

"Gotta hand it to you, you got the respect of every drug dealer up and down the block."

It didn't matter, I had no respect from the people who dumped trash on me every day and damaged my property. I wasn't blaming law enforcement as I knew they could end up in volatile situations resulting in them losing their job which they needed. I couldn't blame the city either as they had lost control just as I had. I didn't blame the Architectural Review Board as their intention is to preserve history which does not work in blighted areas. This city needed change and it needed it fast. When you can no longer enforce the law, our lives are all in danger. It is only a matter of time before this trend moves out of our cities and into the surrounding areas.

7

HOMELESSNESS

2009-2016

Many from out of town brought drugs into Reading which were bought and sold on every corner. Many who are hopelessly addicted, spend their life on disability due to drug abuse and relapse over and over. After the rent money is spent to supply their drug habit they are evicted and left to living on the street. It became more common to see people sleeping on benches throughout the city. Some were more fortunate to have a car to live in.

Every building had a drug dealer living in it supplying the other tenants. I often chased people out of hallways who were sitting on the steps or outside the drug dealer's door waiting for him to come home so they could buy drugs. Most of the buildings had locked front door security doors but that was not a deterrent. They would knock on the window of first floor residents claiming to be a friend visiting one of the tenants. Many mornings during maintenance checks, I would commonly find people sleeping in the hallways where it was warm and dry.

There was another very big problem to homelessness. Where do homeless people go to use a bathroom? Restaurants and corner grocery stores will not allow people to come in off the street to use their bathroom as this only increases their expenses through water usage without taking in revenue. They have to find a place like hallways of apartment buildings or alleyways. I would get calls from tenants that someone had used the hallway as a bathroom that morning and it needs to be cleaned up. Alleyways were also a problem as it made trash pick-up impossible if the alley had been used right before trash pickup arrived. Since the trashmen were unable to access the alleyway to service properties, trash would pile up and owners would be fined by the city for life and safety issues. Complaining to the city only got property owners fined because the mess was our responsibility since it was on our properties. This had to be a violation of environmental laws, but like most of the numerous complaints filed, they just didn't have the manpower to enforce them.

With the amount of trash dumping that occurred every day by the homeless, large numbers of landlords and homeowners were fined. Initially, the city filed in district court against landlords and homeowners for the trash that was dumped on their properties resulting in very high legal costs for the city. To reduce these legal costs, the codes department had their own hearings in city hall where property owners viewed pictures of garbage on their properties that they couldn't move fast enough. The only way to avoid these fines is to do maintenance checks at least three times a day removing the trash as it is dumped. This is impossible for homeowners who are at jobs all day. I was told by the city that if I could find a piece of mail with a name on it in the trash, they would hold them responsible. As I drove by, I saw a man unloading trash bags, mattresses and furniture onto one of my properties. I double parked, jumped out of my car and told him to get rid of it now. He screamed a few obscenities at me and jumped in his pickup truck and took off. I had gotten a license number and reported it to the police. They traced it to another man who loaned it to a number of different people and didn't know who had it at the time the trash was dumped on my property. I took one of the bags of trash, walked into city hall, and dumped it on the counter in the codes department. There were lots of pieces of mail in the bag all from a nine-unit apartment building up the street. Everyone denied dumping the trash. They had a property manager who they suspected of dumping trash and then pocketing the money budgeted for trash. They were unable to locate him as he was in this country illegally and quickly disappeared. They of course, were unable to hold anyone responsible. Something like this happened at least once a week on one of my properties and no one was held responsible but me. It became the cost of doing business.

Problems like these also contributed to the foreclosure rate in the city of Reading. Landlords living out of the area could not do the daily maintenance checks that were required and were not there when tenants received their disability checks. This resulted in lost rents and fines for landlords. Non-paying tenants stayed until they were evicted and after eviction, homeless people took over the building. By law, they also have to be evicted and for many owners, especially the ones who had little money down, it was easier to walk away. I got complaint calls from my tenants about the homeless people who squatted in blighted and vacant buildings disrupting the entire block.

When people move into a city in large numbers, city government scrambles to fill job positions filling them with applicants who perform below average. Landlords complained that they had sent their water bill payment to the treasurer in city hall where it was collected and somehow it was never credited to their account. They received a shut off notice in the mail and ignored it knowing that the bill was paid resulting in their water being shut off. Water shut off in buildings seemed rather routine prompting a code violation and forcing the tenants to find alternate housing. This meant the landlord losing all of his tenants and all of his income forcing him to start over looking for new tenants which became another reason for landlords to give their properties back to the bank.

At the beginning of this chaos, I learned to never take a chance at mailing anything to the city but rather paying city bills such as water, housing permits, and property taxes with a check in person at the treasurer's office downtown in City Hall. I would watch as they credited my payment to my account and then get a date stamped receipt that it was paid. It was important to make sure the check cleared and when it did, I copied both the front and back and stapled it to the stamped receipt. This may sound extreme but if you ever had to spend wasted time proving that you paid a bill that the city claims they never received, you will be glad you did this. It was also important to make sure that your account was credited so your water didn't accidentally get shut off.

I had remembered vividly the day I got a notice from a collection agency in the mail that my school tax on a property was unpaid. At the time, cancelled checks were sent back to us and mine were filed in order by date. The next morning, I went down to the tax office with my cancelled check and they told me that I would now have to deal with the collection agency since it had been sent there. Clearly by the date that they had cashed the check as stamped on the back, they had received my payment during the discount period which meant it was thirty days early. They told me that I would still have to go through the collection agency since it had been sent there and they did not have the ability to handle it. I pointed out to them that there were fees involved since it had been sent to a collection agency which was their error and they should make good on that. No one in city hall was willing to accept responsibility or deal with the problem that they had caused and I was left to deal with a collection agency and paying the extra fees.

8

THE DRUG EPIDEMIC

June 1991

The caller that had just called in for a third-floor apartment sounded too good to be true and tenants for third floor apartments were hard to find. As more and more jobs moved out of the city of Reading, the tenant selection changed from hardworking people to people who were marginally employed with substance abuse problems. If they did have a job, they were low paying jobs considered entry level positions. The problem with many of these types of tenants was that they kept starting over instead of advancing. Many led a life of partying all night and were fired for not showing up to work on time and when they did show up, they were not well rested to perform. They lived pay check to pay check so when the paychecks stopped, they found a friend to live with until they could find another job and save enough money for a first month's rent and security deposit to repeat the cycle all over again. Many were kids from very troubled families with little or no guidance. Many of their parents had lived the same life, never getting ahead and waiting for the day their child turned eighteen and they could throw them out of the house. The role models these children had were low achieving which lead their children to believe that low achievement was the norm and that there was no possibility of anything better.

Not everyone at that time period that lived in the city of Reading fit that profile. Manufacturing still existed for those who were hard working. It was common for the high school graduate to go work at the same plant where his father had worked showing a lot of responsibility at the age of eighteen. For many young people the apartments I rented at the time offered a great start to independence. They were able to live on their own, independent of their parents and save sizeable down payments for homes. They were great buyers because of their steady and good work performance. They did not mix well with those people who wanted to stay up and party all night, so they gradually looked into buying a home as soon as they felt comfortable doing so.

The caller sounded like one of those very responsible people. She was well spoken and able to answer my questions without hesitation and to the point. She had great conversational skills however her answers to my questions pointed more to a marginal type of person. With high hopes and a bad gut feeling, I agreed to meet her and her boyfriend and show them the apartment. They were an attractive couple and he was as well-spoken as she was. They had moved to the area just a few weeks ago and she had already found a job with a local nursing home. He had been born and raised in Reading and they were temporarily staying with his mother in the home where he had grown up until they were able to find an apartment to rent. I took an application from them and called her employer. The employer said that she was being investigated for patient abuse and they were considering firing her. When I called her and told her that her employer gave her a bad reference, she convinced me that this was all a misunderstanding with the employer and assured me that she was still employed with the nursing home. Against my better judgment, I rented the apartment to them.

Within a month, I found out through neighbors, that she was running a call girl operation and meeting men who were pulling up in luxury cars in front of the building. The neighborhood was a relatively nice neighborhood in the northeast section of Reading, where activity like that had never existed. To make matters worse, she had been arrested in the "red light district" for prostitution. She was supporting a heroin habit for both of them, shocking since Reading did not have a heroin problem at that time.

Eventually he left her and she was alone in the apartment when I filed for eviction. During the time that I filed and the time we went to court, she was hospitalized for being beaten and stabbed. The day of court I told the judge that I didn't think that she would be there for the hearing. Just as we were wrapping it up, she ran in apologizing that she was late as she had just been released from the hospital. She showed us the stab wound which I would have never believed it if I hadn't seen it for myself. As we left court together it started to rain and I pulled out an umbrella walking beside her. She told me that her boyfriend had left her and that she had no money and asked if I would give her $5 for at least a sandwich and also a ride on the south east side of the city to a friend's place. As I drove in the opposite direction, I asked her if she had any family she could go to. I had noticed that there was an emergency contact on her application for the apartment when she applied. She insisted that she could not go there. We drove in silence until we arrived at the bus depot. I told her that I was buying her a ticket on the first bus out of Reading. I knew that if she didn't take this chance to get out, someone would find her body dumped on a vacant lot by the next day. She insisted that she would be all right at her friend's house. I turned to her handing her enough money for bus fare and to get something to eat. "I'm going to watch you get on that bus to wherever, just so long that it is leaving Reading, don't come back, you are not safe here." She looked at me for a minute, "hurry, you don't have time to waste," slowly she got out of the car, and turned back. She said, "bless you there is a place in heaven for you" I smiled and said, "I hope so, get the hell out of here now." I watched her get on the bus and I watched the bus leave Reading.

It was obvious to me that she had a troubled life which is how she ended up as a prostitute with a drug problem. Most of the details of their lives were very troubled starting in early childhood. At the time of her eviction in the early 1990's, judges ordered landlords to keep tenant's possessions for at least one year. That meant that personal contents had to be stored somewhere so that the apartment could be rented. I moved their belongings to the basement of that property and eventually, called the numbers on the application hopeful that a relative would pick them up. I got her stepmother on the phone who told me to throw everything out. She told me that she had married her father and had three small children with him. He had divorced her mother when she was young. Her parents shared custody of her and for most of her young life she and her stepmother had problems which led to her leaving home. She met her boyfriend and got hooked on heroin and became a prostitute by the age of sixteen. I met her when she was twenty-three years old. Many like her live this life indefinitely drifting in and out of shelters, treatment, and back to the street. This was pretty much a typical profile of a heroin addict. Heroin was expensive back then and prostitution was the occupation that supported it. For a woman to fall into that life most always was a product of a bad home environment.

June 2012

The typical heroin addict was very different than the addict of twenty years prior. I think the best example of this is Jeff and Helene. At the time that I rented to them they were both in treatment and doing well. They were a married couple with three children all in the custody of her parents. They had owned a home in the suburbs that went into foreclosure around the downtown of the economy in 2009. One day as I sat down in the living room of their apartment, I noticed a picture of a very young girl being embraced by her mother. The girl in the picture was a clean and pretty girl that didn't look much more than twelve years old. Helene told me that was her at age thirteen and her mother when she came out of treatment for the first time. The home that they had lived in was in an old suburban town with nice neat middle class 2300 square foot homes. Her mom had been a stay at home mom and her dad had worked his entire life in a manufacturing job. I had observed a relatively good relationship between Helene and her parents which was not what I typically saw with most heroin addicts.

How did this happen to someone who grew up in a stable household? Jeff and Helene had grown up in the same neighborhood and had known each other their entire lives. This was a neighborhood that most parents would consider an excellent one with a great school district and children the same ages as Jeff and Helene. All of the children in this neighborhood got hooked on heroin between the ages of twelve and fifteen. One of the kids in the neighborhood got a hold of it and they really didn't know what it was. She wasn't sure where it came from but somehow, it ended up in their possession. She was not running from anything unpleasant but she did say the continued use was because of the very peaceful calm feeling that it gave her. This led to her addiction as well as everyone else's in the neighborhood. Both she and Jeff had been through numerous treatment centers over a fifteen year period and seemed to always relapse which is exactly what happened while they were living in my apartment.

They had abandoned their two beloved cats, one left outside to freeze, and the other was hidden away inside a couch. They had sold the keys in the street as well as the stove and refrigerator for pennies on the dollar. I was shocked to find one of the cats living in the sofa to be alive. I was unable to capture it and eventually set a trap for it to be able to get it to an animal shelter so that it could find a home. I used a trap provided to me by the humane society and set a can of cat food in it and left the apartment for the evening. When I came back the next morning the cat was in the trap. It was the most underweight adult cat I had ever seen. I figured it had lived on the water out of the toilet in the apartment but had no food.

Several months later, I got a text message from Helene and a video of me leaving the apartment with the cat in the trap that day. The content of the message indicated that she had no idea that several months had gone by. She thought the eviction had taken place several days before and it was unreasonable of me to remove their cat from the apartment. They assumed that I had removed both cats because it was obvious that they didn't remember leaving the other cat outside in below freezing temperatures. I wondered where they had been for the last several months. Those several months were completely erased from their memory, a common symptom of drug abuse. Long term even after many recovered, they continued to have problems with memory. This caused many to struggle with employment and after going from job after job and failing at all of them eventually they had no choice but to live out the rest of their lives on disability income.

Jeff and Helene had left behind many photo albums of their childhood. It appeared from the pictures, that both had grown up in very normal family settings with many activities. They had been in gymnastics, cheerleading, soccer, baseball and church activities. They both had won some awards and had many certificates among the photos. This was very different from the heroin addict of twenty years ago.

As I thought about the difference, I realized that people most likely to become addicted twenty years ago, went looking for something to self-medicate. Today's heroin addict wasn't looking at all, but drug dealers were coming after victims. As a result, many people unintentionally become hopelessly addicted. It was obvious to me from the number of addicts like Jeff and Helene that I dealt with through property management that drugs were coming into the country in a much bigger way than they did twenty years earlier.

In the 1960's during the Viet Nam war, drugs came into the country but stayed mostly with the servicemen who got hooked overseas. The use otherwise was primarily in the inner cities rarely reaching in neighborhoods beyond that. I remembered in our schools back in the 1970's they had a drug awareness week which meant educating students as young as fifth grade about the terrible effects that drug usage could have on the lives of people. The movies they showed us of drug addicts were so graphic that they would give us all nightmares. How did two nice kids growing up in a great neighborhood get hooked on heroin is a question I found myself asking a lot. They really didn't know the harmful effects of what they were doing. I wondered often what had changed so much in the education of children regarding drug awareness. The movies they showed us back when I was in school would not be allowed to be shown today. They would have a traumatic effect on the students as they did on us resulting in our schools being held liable and risking law suits as we have seen over many trivial matters. It has become too much of a risk for our schools to face. Without showing students the reality of what drugs will do to them, drug awareness education would be useless. As long as students are left uneducated, this leads to a breeding ground for drug dealers to come after innocent people.

As a real estate broker, I saw something else that I had never seen in real estate in prior years, home equity being spent on drug treatment centers for a son or daughter. This put homeowner's lives in jeopardy of losing their home to foreclosure if they had to sell due to a job loss. They did not have enough equity in their home to pay the closing costs to get out which caused many short sales and foreclosures.

After the downturn of the economy in 2009, selling drugs became a means for both old and young to support themselves. Drugs poured into the city at an alarming rate to be bought, sold and used by many. It was very common for a drug dealer to be living in every apartment building supplying all of the tenants in the building with drugs. The shootings resulted when people owed drug dealers money or other dealers infringed upon their territory.

February 2013

I rented to a young man twenty-one years old who had a good job with benefits. He had been employed for two years at the same company never missing a day of work. His employer gave him an excellent reference and for the first year that he lived in my apartment he was an excellent tenant. He paid his rent timely and had just the adequate amount of home furnishings and clothing in the apartment that he needed. That was a good sign that he didn't have spending habits that he couldn't support. He had no visitors other than his brothers who would occasionally stop by very briefly. There was never any loud music or friends running in and out slamming doors and yelling which was the usual complaint that I got involving tenants in that age group.

This all seemed to change overnight. The tenant that lived below him was selling marijuana to mostly college students but did sell other drugs to residents on the block. He began buying marijuana from him and eventually drugs like crystal meth and crack. Because he had a job, he could afford to buy the drugs which attracted all kinds of unemployable, homeless drug addicts. It didn't take long before he was fired from his job and then he had all day to sit around the apartment and get high.

About a half a dozen members of a gang moved into the apartment with him. He no longer had control of his life. When he tried to lock them out, they broke his back exterior door down. They took all of the money that he had saved from his job leaving him with no money to pay his rent or to eat. He called for a pizza delivery and then held up the delivery man who could not identify him because it was late at night and dark. He then became involved in other crimes such as burglaries and purse snatchings. I went to his family and tried to get their help in removing him from the apartment. His parents had gone over a few times and tried to reason with him but were unsuccessful.

He never showed up for the eviction hearing and possession was granted. Five other people occupied the apartment on the day of lockout so I went through the entire process of picking up the order of possession and then paying a constable to lock them all out. The day of lockout, it was snowing and cold. The constable followed me upstairs and while I stood aside, he loudly knocked on the door. He motioned for me to use my key to gain access, and we stepped into the kitchen. The bedroom was the last room in the apartment where six people were sound asleep on dirty mattresses. The constable woke them all up and told them that they could take no more than a few minutes to pack a bag. He stood by while the six of them very zombie like shuffled through mounds of dirty clothing that lay on the floor. I quickly changed the locks and screwed the back door shut that they had kicked in.

Not having any place to go they sat on the steps of vacant buildings in the block while it snowed. Quickly, the tenant's luck ran out. He was arrested for a home invasion several months later that turned violent. While high on drugs, he went to a home of a young mother with two kids. He and another guy knocked on her door and when she opened it, they pushed their way in. He started dumping the contents of drawers in the kitchen looking for money. He ran upstairs and into the young mother's bedroom where he dumped out more drawers. Being concerned for two sleeping young children upstairs she followed him upstairs where he raped her.

In a plea bargain he turned in the tenant who was still living in the apartment below the one that he had occupied for selling drugs. At 5:00am one morning the vice squad kicked in a new front door I had just installed three days earlier. The tenant woke up and most likely knew that they were coming for him. He ran up to the third floor of the building, climbed out a window and ran across the roof tops. That day he was not caught but later turned himself in.

Terrence

I had tenants like Terrence who were selling drugs to supplement their income from another job they held. After manufacturing left many people took other jobs that they weren't always good enough at to keep them employed full time hours. Businesses preferred part time employees to alleviate healthcare due to the rising costs leaving many uninsured. It was common to see many employed at three jobs working about ten hours at each one. I had many tenants like Terrence who were manufacturing workers before manufacturing left Reading. They were model employees who proudly displayed work awards in a frame on their wall for things like perfect attendance or something else work related.

One morning on a maintenance check I found a young man passed out in front of Terrence's apartment door out in the hallway. It was wintertime so he could have been someone who had no connection to anyone residing in the building but just someone who was looking for a warm place to sleep. I leaned down and shook the young man awake and asked him if he was waiting for someone. He said he was waiting for his friend Terrance but when I asked him what Terrence's last name was, he didn't know. He did not fit the description of anyone Terrence would hang out with. After chasing the young man out of the building, I knocked on Terrence's door and told him that someone was sleeping next to his door and asking for him by name. Terrence looked both surprised and a little concerned.

"What did he look like"?

"White, tall, lanky, long hair."

Many like Terrence sold drugs for years discreetly without my knowledge and without being under police suspicion. People like Terrence got into trouble when they started selling drugs to people who are under police suspicion who could eventually give them up in a plea bargain. The young man living above him was a model tenant that evidently Terrence felt safe selling drugs to. When that young man above Terrence committed crimes boldly in the neighborhood Terrence called me and told me about the young man's crimes and suggested that I get rid of him. Between the young man sleeping in the hallway and the phone call I was suspicious of Terrence a tenant that I would not have thought was selling drugs. I told Terrence that an eviction was in process for the tenant above him but there were still thirty days until the tenant was locked out. I hoped for Terrence's sake as well as mine that he had no involvement in the situation above him. I knew that it was just a matter of time until that tenant got into big trouble causing him to give up whoever was selling him drugs in a plea bargain, causing a possible raid which meant damage I would be responsible for.

March 2014

I had a tenant who was so drug addicted many times exhausting her disability income on drugs. Eventually not being able to keep up with her drug habit and rent, I had to evict her. After evicting her and having her removed by a constable, she broke in with people from the street who took over the apartment. Even though there were warning signs plastered all over the windows and doors advising of a $10,000 fine and imprisonment if trespassing, it was not enforced. Police refused to show up and assist for fear of being accused of police brutality and losing their jobs. The city feared lawsuits so the owner was on his own after the legal process was carried out. This left neighborhood blocks having no services of protection that citizens pay for and depend on. The police department hesitated to come down to certain blocks and enforce the law. Eventually buildings become vacant as the neighborhood becomes too dangerous for anyone to be there. The buildings are then taken over by gangs, including people in this country illegally or homeless.

I took matters into my own hands on a Saturday morning when I unscrewed the boards that boarded up the entrance to the apartment. I heard people running out the back door but before doing that they set the wooden fence on fire that sat next to the back door of the apartment. I called the fire department as I watched the fence burn as the flames moved closer to the building. At that moment I realized that there was a better chance that they would not show up. I heard no fire sirens as I watched the fire spread. Orange flames jumped in the air as the fire crackled. No one was coming down to this block as I poured buckets of water on the fire trying to put it out. It was no use. I sat across the street and dialed 911 from my cell phone.

"What is your emergency?'

"I have a seven-unit apartment building on fire. The tenants were evicted and I have an order of possession. They were removed two weeks ago by a constable but keep breaking in and living there. When I tried to take it back, they set the place on fire. "

"What is your location?"

I had already called three times and gave them that information.

"And by the way, this is my third call to you. I know you are not coming down to this block because we haven't had real police protection for years. So while I have you on the phone, I just want to say this, the police and fire department have two choices, they can come down and put the fire out and I will continue to collect rent, or they can ignore my requests and continue to consider this block non-existent and this building will burn down to the ground. So instead of collecting rent, I will collect my policy limits of $750,000, but I believe my carrier may have some questions about this matter for the police and fire department. Either way is fine with me"

I hung up and stared at the flames when off in the distance, I heard sirens. Three fire trucks and four police cars showed up on the block. Every house on that side of the street was condemned and occupied by drug dealers who supplied the block. Blocks like this were bought up by drug lords from either out of state or out of the country. They were bought with cash and were never insured. They caused severe blight on blocks and eventually no insurance carrier wanted anything to do with insuring anything on that block. It was a matter of time before police, fire departments, children protective services, and the codes department became non-existent.

September 2016

I had rented to two guys who had gotten out of treatment for drug and alcohol addiction. They had been in and out of treatment most of their lives for addictions but with drugs being so plentiful their addictions only became worse. They both collected disability income and one had a family member managing that money for him which is how he was able to keep an apartment. No matter how much money he collected in disability, it was never enough to feed his addictions. All kinds of derelicts would come and go in and out of his apartment all day and night to get a shower and crash since they were mostly homeless. One day as I pulled up to the curb in front of the building in which they lived, two police cars pulled up and parked in front of me.

"Welcome to the block officers, glad you stopped, now who might you be looking for," I said.

"We are here on a tip we are not quite sure"

"Well I think I can lead you to the right door."

They hesitated at the front door of the building as we looked down the dark hallway. We entered the dark hallway and hesitated for a second until our eyes adjusted even though the hallway lights stayed on 24/7. They followed me to the top of the stairs and stood behind me as I knocked on the door.

"Who is it"

"Hey guys, it's me, I need to talk to you, open up"

The next thing I knew, the police were handcuffing one of the tenants. When his disability money ran out and he needed more to buy crack, he ripped a TV off the wall in a nearby Laundromat causing it to be unsaleable on the street so he threw it into a nearby dumpster. The owner had a surveillance camera filming the attempted burglary and while running it back, they recognized him and pinpointed an approximate block they believed that he lived in. It was a long shot that they just happened to come down to the block and get him not really knowing who they were looking for.

October 2016

Many children grew up in families where they have lived with abusive, drug addicted parents all of their childhood never being removed from their dysfunctional home. At a very young age, many of these children joined their parents in illegal drugs becoming addicts themselves. I rented an apartment to a mother and daughter which was the case.

At first glance, they seemed to be very ordinary however, both were on disability. Their disabilities turned out to be heroin addiction. On any given day, the mother would sit on the steps out front of the building sobbing with a black eye. She and her daughter would get into a fight that would turn physical. The fighting escalated when the daughter's boyfriend Hermano moved into the apartment. Hermano became violent and kicked in the door to their apartment when mother, daughter or both locked him out. Everyone was so high on drugs that they didn't really remember how it happened. The police showed up to lock up Hermano after someone called them. The violence escalated while mother and daughter blamed each other for Hermano going to jail. Of course, it is my responsibility to replace the door immediately at my expense since they have no security. They apologized promising that this would never happen again. The mother blamed Hermano for everything and the daughter blamed the mother. Things seemed quiet for a few weeks until the mother and another tenant down the hall overdosed and were taken to the hospital. There was constant traffic in the building and it was difficult to determine whether the drugs were coming from the dealing of another tenant or someone outside. Two people overdosing on the same day seemed likely that they got a bad strain of something. Both tenants were saved but needed long term care in nursing care facilities paid by Medicaid. The daughter informed me that the state had taken back her mother's disability check and food stamps because of her care in a state facility. She added that this was nothing to worry about because Hermano, who also got a disability check for drug addiction would be getting out of prison and moving in with her to help her out. I told her that he was not allowed back in the apartment after kicking the door down. I filed for eviction and the daughter and a girlfriend showed up in court. They told the judge that the friend's parents owned a very successful restaurant in New York and had agreed to help them out with the rent. I continued with the eviction process knowing that it would not work out the way the friend said. I had been through this so many times to know better.

Five days later I got a call from another tenant in the building who told me that drugs were being sold out of the unit at all hours of the day and night. A dangerous gang had invaded the apartment and had taken it over. The tenant below them called me to tell me that there was leaking coming from that apartment which gave me an excuse to check it out for myself. A gang member was guarding the door as I walked over the threshold. Both girls were in bed in a fog like drug trance. Hermano sat on the couch with another gang member standing guard over him. It appeared that there was a leaking toilet seal. I knew that no one would want to spend any time in there to do a repair under the circumstances. I asked the gang member guarding the door if I could talk with Hermano outside. He motioned for another gang member to follow us outside and stand guard. We walked across the street and stood at the parking authority. I told the other guy to keep his distance so we could talk. He reluctantly stayed across the street on the steps of the building, nervously glancing our way from time to time as we talked.

Hermano told me that they were all being held hostage in the apartment by gang members. The police knew about it because he had made a deal with them to help get the illegals that are camping out there in exchange for a lighter sentence. The police couldn't get in without probable cause and a search warrant. It sounded to me like they were not going to leave until a constable removed them. The only way the hostage situation would end he informed me, is through an eviction by me. I told him that I had filed and it was in the process, but it looks like he will have to sit there for eleven more days and endure whatever horrors were taking place in that apartment. I was just thankful that there were no children involved. Hermano was not aware of how a legal eviction worked and thought that I could just tell them all to leave and it was over. I explained the legal process to him which takes about forty-five days if everything goes perfectly, and has been in the process with eleven days left. With that, the tears rolled down this grown man's cheeks. As he wiped them away, I tried to guess his age. It was always difficult to tell with the years of drug addiction people suffered. While he was in prison, his girlfriend had spent her entire disability check that month on heroin and it wasn't enough. She allowed gang members into her apartment in exchange for more. I saw it over and over with so many people. As long as they were around anyone dealing drugs, they were unable to ever be clean. They were always caught in this vicious cycle of rehab and relapse.

On the day of the eviction, two constables and I went over to find the door open and no one inside. I worked quickly to change the locks as the two constables were looking around. As I changed the lock one constable said, "Hey, this gal changes locks faster than any locksmith in this town." I turned my head to face them and said, "I have had a lot of practice at changing locks, probably as much or more than any locksmith in this town has had." No sooner did I say that Hermano and his girlfriend came back. Both constables were armed and quickly reached for their guns in their holsters. They held onto them as they remained in the holster and both moved in front of me to block the door. One of them bellowed "stop right there and don't cross this threshold." Hermano gave them a pathetic look and said, "May we just come in and get a bag, we will be living in the street and just need one bag each." I nodded to the constable and told him it wasn't a problem for me if they both packed one bag. The constable looked back at them and said, "One bag, five minutes and no more." After Hermano and his girlfriend left the constable turned to me. I was finished changing the lock and he asked, "Are we done here"? "No, we are not", I answered. Both constables looked puzzled. The street is a dangerous place for these people to be. I believe they will be back to take over the apartment, the No Trespassing sign with the threat of prison means nothing to these people. They have served most of their adult life in prison. Doesn't matter to them where they live in this apartment, the street or prison, so what do you suggest when you leave and they resume living here", I asked the constables. "Call the police." I had been there before. The police did everything not to come down to this block and have a confrontation.

Within ten minutes after I had left the property, I received an anonymous phone call from someone I did not know informing me that the gang members who had taken Hermano and his girlfriend hostage had broken back into the apartment. I immediately dialed the police and the dispatcher told me that she would send the police immediately but I would have to meet them there. I turned around back towards the city and the building that I had just left. I arrived along with four squad cards and eight police officers. They were already making arrests and handcuffing people. That included the girl whose parents owned a restaurant in New York, the gang member that watched while I spoke to Hermano that day, and five Mexican men who were in this country illegally but wanted for violent crimes according to the constables who also came back. The ring leader that answered the door the day I went to check on the leak was the most wanted and had gotten away. I watched the officers throw the illegal men into a van that had also showed up.

Later that evening, I settled in to watch one of the presidential debates between Donald Trump and Hillary Clinton. Donald Trump was talking about the drugs pouring into this country and building a wall. The afternoon's fiasco was still fresh in my mind when Donald Trump said, we have some bad hombres in this country and we need to put them on a train and send them right on out of here. Every day for ten years I saw the city of Reading in a state of crises due to bad hombres violating innocent people. The police were wasting their time trying to get justice for those victims due to the fact that the criminals were not in our criminal system. They could not afford to spend time investigating a crime with no suspects and the criminals long gone, leaving the country. I thought of the anguish I felt every time I tried to reach out to a government agency asking for help for someone who desperately needed it like children caught in the middle of drugs and violence. I thought of the frustration of dealing with city government that had lost control because of illegal immigration and the migration of criminals from mostly New York as well as Mexico. I thought of the fear of the drugs that seemed to be endlessly pouring into our city and finding their way to surrounding suburbs.

October 2016

I knew it was coming and it was what kept me awake for the last eight years at night. The only thing separating me and the city with the problems that increased rapidly was the Penn Street bridge. The suburban neighborhoods were great places to live but they wouldn't stay that way if there wasn't change in the inner city they surrounded. I feared for the day when the inner-city problems would eventually move to those surrounding areas.

I had received a letter from the electric company regarding installing a new meter and asking to make sure that there was adequate room for the installer to work. That side of the house was forgotten about as there were no windows and it was easy to sometimes forget that the landscaping needed to be trimmed and maintained. Early one morning I went out with some lawn bags and started trimming and cleaning out. I bent down to scoop the dead leaves from the previous fall when I found it there in my own yard.

Many arrests had been made as carloads of white powder had come into the city by large drug lords who redistributed it to smaller dealers who in turn redistributed to small street dealers. They identified blocks where illegal drugs were sold by hanging a pair of sneakers on electrical wires overhead. It was common to see this on most blocks in inner cities. Some identified themselves by standing on corners in front of small grocery stores all day and well after dark. We still had time before the drug epidemic reached the suburbs or so I thought, but with each passing day, I saw suburban children who had been caught in the hopeless addiction of heroin along with general use of other drugs.

I slowly turned over the small baggie that I had just found in my landscaping. I would think nothing of this if I were on the other side of the bridge where I saw these little baggies every day on the street, inside apartments as well as the hallways in the buildings I managed. As I stared at the baggie in my hand, I searched my mind as to who would have dropped it there. Often, I had noticed kids walking home from school that were not of driving age yet cutting through my yard. I would see them walk though my backyard and turn the corner to this side of the house with no windows. It would be discreet enough for them to snort the white powder while walking home from school and then toss the little baggie into my landscaping to be assured that they were not bringing any evidence home in their backpacks. Their parents would have no idea until they were helplessly hooked. They would spend years in treatment only to continually relapse. Their parents could not live with them and their hopeless addictions and after receiving disability for them, would rent them a cheap apartment in the city. Many of these parents became responsible for raising the children their children produced. Drug treatment was primarily paid for by Medicaid which was further draining our health care costs. What was so common in the inner city was now moving to the suburbs evidenced by that little baggie. Health care costs can go nowhere but upward as the drug epidemic expands to the suburbs and would keep going if not stopped at our borders.

Police Protection

Illegal drug use causes many other problems in our society. Some of the symptoms of illegal drug use are crime, prostitution, child abuse, and escalating health care costs. Eventually drugs will capture people in a trap that they can't get out of. Neighborhoods can be taken over by drugs and people so hopelessly addicted that services such as police, the fire department and child protective services will check out. You will find yourself as a property owner calling repeatedly for those services that will not respond to your calls. During the election of 2016, it was not considered safe for anyone but a black police officer to come down and answer crime in a predominantly black block. That had never been the case before. The police department realizes that people on drugs can be dangerous acting irrationally and placing the police in a bad position. If they don't have a black police officer to answer the call, it goes unanswered. In those neighborhoods where I managed property it was so obvious when I called the police department and they asked for a description of the criminal immediately. If I didn't talk about race, they would ask me. "Are we talking about a white man, Hispanic, black?" Many officers just couldn't risk coming down to the block where they may have to shoot in self-defense only to be suspended when they have a family to support. Many police officers were scared to come down to blocks where they had no idea who these gangs were that had taken over buildings. It was the equivalent of stepping into a war zone which was not what they signed up for when they became police officers.

On the corner of the building was a constant active prostitution trade where prostitutes openly waited for their customers to pick them up in a vehicle. If their customers showed up on foot or on a bicycle, they routinely used my hallway. It was common to hear me yell, "Hey, stop right there, I'm going to have to collect rent from you for occupying my hallway." They would be shocked because the building had been vacant for years after going back to the bank several times before I bought it.

Many people who are addicted to drugs and alcohol are on disability income which feeds their habit until they run out of that money. When they run out of money before their next disability check they will turn to crime.

9

CRIME

The absence of manufacturing jobs caused an increase in crime as many manufacturing workers became permanently unemployed. This perpetuated the downward spiral in families with children growing up with one parent involved in criminal activity. This set a bad example for many men to grow up to be unproductive, unemployable, and often criminals. Most were born to young single women with an uninvolved father. Neither parent having the financial means to raise a child along with being raised in a dysfunctional family increased their odds of repeating the cycle. Mothers were left to try to finish their education and make a living for themselves and their child, while their parents raised that child as well as others that were born after. As soon as their children were old enough to stay home alone after school, they did so while they wasted time playing video games instead of doing homework or being involved in after school activities.

Video games take up a lot of time and prevent anyone from truly focusing on directing their life in a forward direction and in any true goal setting. They were a popular pastime with many school aged kids that continued into adult life. It was easy for them to drift into a lifestyle of crime and drugs since they had a lot of idle time and little responsibility.

By the time they were old enough to get a part time job while still in school, they instead chose to go home to video games and hanging out with their friends. That left them well behind those children who did get those part time jobs while in high school. Instead of learning skills on the job, they slipped further and further behind. Many start out with small petty crime and if they don't find positive influences in their lives usually through a parole officer their crimes continue and become more serious.

Many of these small crimes do not go to trial but are settled through plea bargaining. The defendant agrees to plead guilty to a lesser charge or less charges through the recommendation of the district attorney and the prosecution agrees to accept that to avoid going to trial. As their crimes become more serious over time, their chance of plea bargaining becomes less leaving their fate in the hands of a jury. Some are lucky enough to get off the first few times due to lack of enough evidence or jurors who don't make good decisions. Many of the best people who would make the best decisions as jurors are the first to ask to be excused because of the busy lives that that they lead.

Far more criminals go free versus being wrongly convicted, however someone who has never been around criminals or criminal activity are likely to think the opposite. They hear about that one case in the news where someone is wrongly convicted but never hear about the thousands of cases where the jury failed to come up with a unanimous decision to convict a criminal. This explains how a violent criminal can be found innocent only to be released back into society to become a repeat offender.

Beyond a reasonable Doubt

Three young men considered to be social outcasts at their high school hung out together skipping school and getting into mischief. As time went on, the mischief escalated into burglarizing homes in the community while the occupants were away for the day at work. They were finally apprehended when a witness came forward.

They had chosen to break into one of the young men's former girlfriend's parents' home. The witness, a neighbor, observed them driving by her home at 11:00am. The witness's home was located on a dead-end street therefore the young men had no other reason to be on the street but to visit the former girlfriend. Several months prior, the girl's parents had intervened in the relationship encouraging her to break it off with this young man who was going nowhere fast. The neighbor was curious realizing that she had not seen these young men since the break up and also had never observed them in the neighborhood at that time of day when everyone was at work. As they drove by, the neighbor recognized the familiar pickup truck that the former boyfriend always drove as well as the former boyfriend driving it. Twenty minutes later they drove down the street with several TV's in the bed of the truck. She observed one of the friends sitting in the passenger seat as they drove by leaving the neighborhood. The third friend was sitting in the front seat between the driver and the passenger. My father was a juror for the third man's trial.

It is the job of the defense attorney to create doubt in the juror's minds that would lead to an acquittal. It is the responsibility of jurors to be able to think rationally and recognize that is what a defense attorney's job is and to be able to see beyond that.

The defense attorney asked the witness if she could identify the defendant and she pointed him out in the courtroom. He then asked her if she saw his face as they drove by the day her neighbor's home was robbed and she said she had not because his long blond hair was covering his face. Upon cross examination, the prosecuting attorney asked the witness if the two already convicted young men had another friend with a similar off the beaten path look of long blond hair past his shoulders. The witness said that she had never observed these three with anyone else but each other. In further testimony it was revealed that these three young men always wore the same clothes every day and that the young man sitting in the middle was wearing the same blue jacket that the defendant always wore.

My father said that there was never a doubt in his mind that this defendant was guilty. It seemed like an easy case to decide. When the jurors all filed into the deliberation room it became apparent very quickly that they were all in agreement that the defendant was guilty except for one very young juror. She said that she could not be 100% sure that the defendant wasn't the same person as the person sitting between the other two in the pickup truck because the witness testified to never having seen his face. Slowly, one by one the jurors caved in with my father being the last to cave in even though they all believed that the defendant was guilty beyond a reasonable doubt. When I asked him why he caved in, he said that if he didn't, the defendant would be retried again with a different jury wasting everyone's time and the taxpayer's money to possibly come up with the same outcome. He believed that the other jurors felt the same way and believed that it was impossible to educate this young juror on what "beyond a reasonable doubt" meant. People like this juror do not have enough life experiences as well as not enough experience in making good decisions. No one wants to sit in deliberations for hours while this one juror lacks understanding of what beyond a reasonable doubt means.

Even though my father was unhappy with the outcome he said that these particular young men didn't harm anyone bodily or murder anyone, and that the things they stole are not as important as lives.

Mistaken Identity

As the jury selection progressed in the criminal case that was about to be heard, I became sure that I would not be selected. It appeared that the jurors who were being selected by both the prosecution and the defense fit very similar profiles. As much as that didn't make sense in itself, the jurors selected were predominately black or Hispanic and female. After ten jurors had been selected, the prosecuting attorney, a white female and the defense attorney, a black male, stood together looking over the list. My number was called along with a black male by the defense attorney. A Hispanic female alternate was called by the prosecuting attorney.

The plaintiff, a Hispanic female, took the stand and testified that the defendant had broken into her home in the middle of the night, dragging her and her four children out of bed. He tied the four children up and beat and raped their mother. As the testimony became graphic, one juror started to throw up. She was removed and replaced with the alternate. I fought with the other jurors to hold back my tears as the room in front of me blurred. As the tears flowed down my cheeks with the rest of the jurors, I found the defense attorney glancing at me from time to time, and then something really indescribable happened that made no sense to me at all. He smiled at me.

I had managed property in the city for years and was known by city agencies to be an advocate for woman and children. The defense attorney being from legal aid had to know that and had to know that I would not be beneficial at all to his case considering that it was a case that not only involved a rape victim, but also her children. It was puzzling to me that he would choose me as a juror.

It was established during testimony that the defendant was wearing a ski mask but the plaintiff knew it was him. She had met him on an online dating site and briefly dated him but broke it off when he became controlling and abusive. She recognized his voice, his hands, his scent, and testified that there was no doubt in her mind that it was him.

The defendant, a very well dressed, good looking man, insisted that he was not the rapist. His testimony was very believable and he appeared to be credible. He kept insisting that she had the wrong man and of course, no one wants to convict an innocent man.

The defendant's parole officer was called to the stand with a file that was six inches thick. It was determined through his testimony, that this defendant had many prior rape allegations but had not ever been convicted. I was shocked that the defense attorney was not objecting to the testimony of the parole officer which had nothing to do with the case being heard. After enough testimony to remove all doubt, the defense attorney said "maybe I should be objecting to this."

"It's too late for that" responded the judge.

There was very little deliberation. We were all completely in agreement that the defendant was guilty. When the guilty verdict was delivered, the defendant was shocked and continued to exclaim his innocence.

Eventually I figured out how that case was really won. The defense handed the defendant to the prosecution. They had as close to a perfect jury as they could get. Even though the defense allowed testimony from the parole officer that made the case, there are still people who can't make a decision. There are still jurors who would find the defendant not guilty and that is how violent criminals go free.

I can't begin to imagine how any woman or anyone for that matter could go to endless ends of the earth to defend a rapist. Until you sit on a jury and listen to the graphic description it's difficult for me to imagine how any human being could lack enough compassion to really defend a case like that one.

10

SEXUAL ASSAULT

I have heard the details from about a dozen or so sexual assault victims that lead up to the actual assault. All assaults involved a person they knew along with drugs, alcohol or some illegal activity they were involved in. Many admitted later that their judgment was really bad that put them in a position to be assaulted. This is what makes so many sexual assault allegations difficult to prove.

Internet and Sexual Assault

During a city codes inspection in southeast Reading we found a basement with a bedroom set up consisting of a bed, night tables, a chest of drawers, a table and two chairs and a pool table. The first floor had access to the basement which they claimed that they were using for storage. That was believable as I couldn't imagine that anyone would want to sleep in this particular basement. The walls were stone and mortar that was deteriorated and dirt was falling all over the furniture. The first indication of a problem was in the middle of the summer when the second-floor tenant told me that there were young women in the backyard threatening to call the police. They were well dressed driving luxury cars with out of state license plates. The next call came in the fall of that same year from the same tenant. She said that she had woken up to what she thought was a woman being attacked and was nervous since her husband worked nights leaving her home alone. I told her there was nothing I could do unless she could be more specific. The next call came from the tenant's husband, several weeks later. He told me that a woman had been seen running out of the basement screaming at 2:00am and half dressed. He thought she may have been raped but not sure. He told me that he couldn't have this going on with his wife home alone and felt that I needed to do something. I really doubted that any of us would get to the bottom of this but in order to cover myself from any liability of not making an attempt at taking action, I picked up the phone and called a detective friend in the police department. If anything happened, he could vouch for me that I did all I could in taking action by reporting the incident to the police. He told me he had been on vacation, just returning to work that morning and he would see if anything had been reported and call me by the end of his shift at 3:00pm. He called me back in ten minutes.

There had been a sexual assault reported in that block by an employee of a convenience store at the end of the block claiming that a half-dressed woman had entered the store claiming to have been assaulted. She didn't know which house in the block that this had occurred and the police came up empty handed when they did a neighborhood canvass. There had been a serial rapist in that area for ten years matching the description that she gave the police. I told my detective friend that I believe he is a friend of my tenants who had been hanging around that building for about ten years and spending a lot of time overnight and probably sleeping in the basement. He was not on the lease and I didn't believe that it was his residence because I had never seen a piece of mail come to that building addressed to him. The police detective said that they had talked to the residents at that particular address who said it was just two guys living there and they had both been asleep for hours and didn't hear a thing. Neither guy matched the description that the victim gave the police. They asked me to come to police headquarters and take a look at a mug shot book to see if I could identify him. It took about five minutes to pick him out. The police officer asked me if I was sure. Over the years, I had half a dozen conversations with him or so standing within three feet of him. There wasn't a doubt in my mind.

This particular street was very busy with no street lights on that side of the street. Apparently, the incidents were occurring with more frequency than ever due to him advertising on a dating site and drawing young women from all over. This would explain the young women in the backyard the previous summer with out of state license plates. He would meet them in a bar close to the apartment. They would be confused if they were unfamiliar with the area so he would offer to walk them to their car. He would then walk them by the apartment and tell them that he just had to feed his cats and it will only take a minute. They would follow him into the basement where the attack would take place. Now, they finally could identify and charge him since the victim had picked the same mug shot as I had.

There were several conversations that went on between me and my detective friend as he called me to ask more questions. I got a call from the tenant who originally complained to tell me that the perpetrator had moved out of the basement and down the street to City Park where he was living in a gray car that he had borrowed. My tenant was very upset that the police had not apprehended him and predicted he would disappear making any arrest impossible. A few days later my detective friend called me to thank me for my cooperation but the victim had dropped the charges.

"I can't believe that she would drop the charges when we have identified the rapist."

"This was not a rape case because no actual rape happened however that is just a small part of it. Most victims don't want to testify as they have to testify detail by detail of exactly what happened and that can get uncomfortable."

"I understand that but by not testifying she is putting other women in danger." He's free to continue sexually assaulting women."

"His story is very different than hers."

"Of course it is."

"It's not only that, but the fact that we quickly came up with some things in her background that will definitely come up in a trial that she does not want made public. When it's all said and done, there is no guarantee that we will get a conviction."

"If that is the case, how does anyone ever get

convicted"?

"These cases are extremely difficult. Unfortunately, the victims usually make bad witnesses, they have a lot of problems themselves that are brought forth in testimony and many times get criminals off. We need a good witness that is credible and they are far and few between. Over the years, there had been numerous rapes reported where the rapist fits the description of what you and the victim have picked out of the mug shot book. We have called two of the best victims and have asked if they would come in and also look at the mug shot book and they have declined to do so. They know that the next step would be to testify as a witness and they don't want to do that. They have built new lives, have married and have children and their families may not know that this happened to them and they wish to keep it that way. That is usually how it happens with those that would make the best witnesses. They just don't wish to dredge up the past and make it public. "

What happened to the perpetrator? He left the area until this incident blew over and then came back six months later and continued to hang around.

Drugs and Sexual Assault

I had rented several apartments to a woman for ten years and got to know her fairly well. She was the person that tipped me off if someone was violating terms of their lease agreement. Being in her fifties, and having children when she was very young, they were grown and long gone so it was just her and a common law husband. She had lived on welfare all of her life and her husband worked full time. Never once did I have any problems with them as they paid the rent on time and did not do anything that required my attention.

One day, I noticed that I hadn't seen him around for at least a few months. I asked her what happened to him and she didn't offer any details except that he went back to Mexico. She got on a dating site where she met a much younger and handsome man. Before long he moved in and I got complaint calls from the other tenants. They would sit up all night outside either in the front of the building or on the roof drinking quart size bottles of malt liquor and hard liquor. If they were sitting out front, they would hang a trash bag on the railing to collect the empty bottles. If I didn't get around to a maintenance check before the city codes office opened, I would get fined for the trash not being disposed of properly. She would promise that it would not happen again and that she would move the trash around to the back after they were done sitting outside but somehow that never happened and I continued to get fined. One evening while driving by the building, I saw them with a few of his friends, sitting on the roof smoking, drinking and laughing loudly. It clearly stated in all leases that no one was allowed on the roof and when I spoke to her about it the next day, she denied that they were on the roof. I told her that I had driven by and had seen her on the roof and she continued to deny it. I believe that she had no recollection of the night before. After several months of this she answered the door on a rent collection day with a black eye. She said she would be late with the rent because her boyfriend had to leave and she had a PFA on him.

"What happened"

"I don't know"

"What do you mean you don't know did you guys have a fight or something?"

"No, he just went crazy and beat me up, he cracked several of my ribs and repeatedly punched me all over which is how I got this black eye."

"Come on, there has to be a reason that he beat you up, something must have pissed him off"

"I have no idea"

Things quieted down after he left. She said there were too many bad memories in the apartment and asked if I would move her to the first floor that became available. After moving and getting caught up with her rent, I thought all of the drama was over and she would go back to being a model tenant. There had always been family members coming and going but no one living with her. She continued to get onto dating sites looking for someone but didn't bring anyone home to live with her.

One month when I showed up to collect the rent, I found her apartment completely empty. This was common for tenants to do if they were unable to pay their rent but unusual for this tenant. The apartment was completely clean and I rented it immediately. Several months went by when I drove by and saw her sitting out front on a lawn chair as if she still lived there. Over the next several weeks I would see the same thing and she would stare at me blankly as I drove by. One evening I got out of my car on a maintenance check and said to her,

"Wow, you certainly left in a hurry."

She stared blankly at me. There were several people standing around and one sitting and talking with her.

"Can I speak to you a minute, privately." she asked

"Sure"

It was evening around dusk as we walked to the end of the street and stood on the corner. It didn't appear that anyone was in ear shot of us.

"Hey, I'm really sorry that I left in a hurry but I had to, you see, I was raped in your apartment."

I felt my heart skip a beat as my mind raced trying to understand how this could have happened and wondered if I overlooked something that made me liable. The building had just gone through a codes inspection and passed. All windows and doors had secure locks on them.

"How did he get in?" I asked.

"I let him in."

I breathed a sigh of relief knowing then it was someone she knew and not some serial rapist that entered through a window or door with a broken lock.

"Who was it?" I asked

"My former boyfriend's son."

"Which boyfriend?"

"The one who went back to Mexico."

"How old is he?"

"Twenty"

"Where does he live?"

"A block away, you know him he stayed here sometimes when his father and I lived together."

I was starting to feel sick to my stomach and wondering how something like this could happen.

"Where did you move to?"

"Living in my car."

I glanced over at her car parked a few feet from where we stood and noticed piles of trash bags and boxes jammed into the car. A few kitchen pot handles stuck out of a box on top of piles of other boxes.

"Did you report this rape?"

"Yes, I did and I'm pressing charges. He's going to jail, that's for sure, I'm not backing down. They did a rape kit and assigned me a rape counselor."

"How did this happen?"

"He and his girlfriend had a big fight and he called and asked if he could stay here for the night because she threw him out. When he called, I was already in bed asleep and told him I would get up and unlock the security door and my door so that he could let himself in. "

"What time was this?"

"I don't know, it was dark and I had fallen asleep earlier."

"What time did you fall asleep?"

"I'm not sure I was drinking all day and just kind of passed out."

"Well, was it 6pm, 8pm, 10pm about what time,"

"I have no idea."

"Well, if you left all of the doors open, anyone could

have come in."

"No, it was definitely him, I woke up when he came in, he told me that he had just scored some crack and was smoking it. We passed this pipe back and forth and I don't remember anything after that until 1:00pm the next day. No doubt that this crack was laced with something because this never happened to me before."

"So how do you know you were raped."?

"I can tell, I just know."

"If you don't remember anything, how do you know"?

"Because I woke up with no pajama bottoms on"

"Is there a chance that you took them off but don't remember doing so"

"No, I wouldn't do that I always sleep with pajama bottoms on"

"When he left, did he lock the doors?"

"I have no memory of him leaving but I would assume that he did."

"Did you talk to him about this at all"?

"No, I just pressed charges."

A short time later she came up with a security deposit and first month's rent and moved into another apartment I had available at that time. I watched this tenant become angrier and angrier as nothing happened with her case. I can't imagine after listening to these facts that anyone was going to bring this case to trial. She was under the impression that a DNA test would be performed to establish that it was him but what does that prove? With both of them being under the influence of a drug laced with who knows what, no matter what either one of them says, neither is a credible witness.

She complained constantly about every other tenant in the building and expected me to make them speak more quietly as their loud talking drove her out of her mind. She gave her therapist permission to speak to me and she reiterated what my tenant already had told me regarding the noise level in the building. Her behavior became bizarre and quite unusual from all of the ten years that I had known her as a tenant. She eventually moved out without leaving a forwarding address.

Several other Assaults

I heard several other stories from sexual assault victims. Some reported and some that go unreported. They had long histories of drug abuse and one admitted to supporting her habit through prostitution. This is a risky occupation to be involved in, and as much as no one deserves to be sexually assaulted the risk of that for a prostitute is much greater. Two different women told me of stories of being kidnapped, having no idea what town or where they ended up other than a basement in a house. One was a prostitute and the other was trying to buy drugs.

While the prostitute was negotiating with a customer who she did not know, another guy came up behind her, grabbed her and threw her in the trunk. She said they drove for about forty-five minutes and she was blind folded when they removed her from the trunk and carried her through a basement entry in the ground and into a dirt basement. After being raped by both of them, she was tied to a basement pole and they left. She managed to break free and escape through the same entry door where she came in to step out into an area of acres of vacant land around her. There was a farm house off in the distance that she walked to and knocked on the door for help only to have the door opened by one of her captors. She was brought back to the basement where she was beaten and tied up again. She believes that she was held captive for a total of about three or four days when she managed to escape again. This time she walked for hours until she came upon a town with a population and a main road of businesses. She walked into a fast-food restaurant where employees called the police. The police were unable to make an arrest in this case as she did not know who her captors were or where they lived. They tried to get a general area of the location where this had occurred by estimating how long she had walked and in what direction she came from but came up with no leads. There had been no other reports of anything in any of the areas in which she could have been. Since both times that she had escaped it had been dark, she had no description of the house, street signs or any other landmarks.

The other case was a young woman and her girlfriend trying to buy drugs. A man only known to them by a street name lured them to a basement where he said that there was a party going on and the drugs would be free. He drove them to an upscale home in a neighboring county late at night. Even though the home was dark, it never occurred to either one that anything was wrong until they got into the basement where the party consisted of only three other guys. The girls were tied up and gang raped and when one screamed, rags were stuffed into their mouths. All of a sudden there were sirens heard in the distance and the four guys took off out of the outside basement entry door. The neighbors hearing a scream had called the police. The home was a vacant home in a suburban neighborhood owned by the bank.

The policed investigated the previous owners learning that they had no involvement. They questioned neighbors who said that there had been no activity in that house until that evening. The police had nothing to go on except a man with a street name which led nowhere.

Interview with a Rapist

This chapter would not be complete without an interview with the other side, a rapist. When I was in my early twenties, I worked with a man who admitted that he had been involved in a gang rape and murder for which he served fifteen years in prison. It made sense to me then why this man who at age thirty-eight had just gotten married two years ago. In conversations with him I was finding constant blanks in his life almost like he had dropped out of society for a long time. The fact that he was incarcerated for fifteen years made perfect sense. He had come from a home of dysfunction and at a young age got involved in a violent gang whose primary activity was manufacturing and selling illegal drugs when they found themselves in a dispute with another gang. He and another gang member were ordered by their leader to kidnap a rival gang's girlfriend and hold her hostage while torturing her. He blamed heavy drug use and being under the influence at the time of the rape and murder of the girl. He took a plea bargain in exchange for information about his partner as well as other information about the illegal activities of the gang. He had great remorse for what he had done and was haunted by it every day of his life. He often wished he could go back and undo this awful crime. He said that fifteen years in prison gave him a long time to think about this crime, find religion, and turn his life around.

11

CHILD ABUSE

Neighbors, teachers, pediatricians, and property managers are a few people who may come in contact with children that may be abused. Because it is nearly impossible for a child to escape an abusive situation without help, they need these people to alert Child Protective Services so that they can make a determination as to whether or not that child is safe.

What causes a person to be an abuser? Many counselors who specialize in that field say that the abuser feels very much out of control of their life. Many make poor life choices resulting in the need for alcohol and drugs in an attempt to self-medicate. Over time, routine use of alcohol and drugs lead to mental illness causing dysfunctional family relationships and child abuse.

It is not up to us to decide whether or not a child is suffering from child abuse but it is also not an excuse for ignoring the suspicions that we as citizens sometimes have. Agencies such as Child Protective Services have trained counselors who will investigate complaints made anonymously and decide on appropriate action to be taken. Most cases are referred for family counseling or parenting classes. Serious cases are removed from their homes and placed in the foster care system. We as citizens have to become strong advocates for children and do everything possible to facilitate provisions for safe havens for them. One phone call may not be enough, but several follow up calls may be necessary due to agencies generally suffering from case overload along with budget restraints. If children are left in their abusive homes for their entire childhood and are lucky enough to survive, they have a slim chance of becoming successful functioning adults.

Through property management I came in contact with children who were abused by their parents. I either witnessed it myself or had taken complaints from neighbors. I would tell the abuser that they need to get into counseling as soon as possible or I will call Child Protective Services. I believe that saved a lot of children from the abuse escalating and maybe even saved their lives. At least they were in the hands of a therapist whose expertise was dealing with child abuse.

Talking with the abuser was not always the answer and became the cases that needed to be reported immediately so that the child or children can be removed as soon as possible. These are the worst cases that usually involve drug and alcohol addiction. Drugs have played a major part in violence that occurs in our country with parents who even sometimes have great remorse for what they did to their children while under the influence.

June 1998

Many times, children end up in the foster care system because there are no other family members suitable to raise the children. I found that drug and alcohol addiction was often a family affair running through generations of families with many falling through the cracks.

One of my apartments was occupied by a husband and wife in their mid-fifties. It was a second marriage for both having no children together but she had eight grown children from prior relationships. Their rent was paid from the disability check they received every month due to alcohol addiction. Both spent the day in bed with the TV blasting while drinking themselves into oblivion until they passed out for the rest of the day only to wake up the next day to start the cycle again. I collected their rent on the third of the month needing to arrive early in the morning before the next drinking cycle began. Eventually they were assigned to a nursing home under Medicaid. A caseworker helped clean and move them out of the apartment leaving a stack of paperwork beside a trash can outside. The trash company did not consider it properly discarded and refused to take it. I bent down by the stack and started to bag it up before throwing it in a trash receptacle when my eye caught legal paperwork to remove a grandchild from their custody. The child had previously been removed from her daughter's care. While under the daughter's care, the child was found by a doctor to have numerous fractures in different stages of healing. The grandmother stepped up and filed for custody of the child which was granted. Due to their alcohol addiction the child was neglected resulting in severe malnutrition. At the age of twenty-two months, the child was found to weigh only thirteen pounds. They fought to keep custody of the child for the money they received from the state for acting as foster parents, but did eventually lose custody.

May 1999

I rented an apartment to a young mother with a two-year old daughter who worked and had part time custody of her child. This young mother had been in treatment for drug and alcohol addiction and was in parenting classes so that she could regain full custody. When she did regain full custody, she promptly relapsed. On the day the rent was due, I went over to the apartment to find the door wide open and two toddlers left unattended in the apartment. The apartment was filthy with mounds of dirty dishes laying around, left-over food piled on some of the dishes with bugs crawling through it. The two toddlers, one belonging to a friend and the other hers, were screaming as they ran back and forth in dirty diapers that hadn't been changed in days. Both toddlers' legs were red and blistered from fecal matter running down their legs and not being cleaned. The mother was a prostitute out supporting a drug habit. No child should be left alone in an apartment let alone be so neglected that their needs are obviously not being met. I called Child Protective Services and the children were promptly removed from her care. The mother left the apartment for good and entered into another treatment program.

After she finished, treatment, she moved into another apartment on the other side of town with a man recently released from prison. She had met him through letter writing, the letters all left behind when she left my apartment. Within a year he shot her in the back of the head killing her during a violent domestic dispute. Before meeting her, he had served time in prison for throwing his infant son against a wall and killing him when he wouldn't stop crying.

Child abuse does not always occur in children's homes by their parents or other family members but also occurs with people who parents have trusted to care for their children. I rented to various tenants over the years who worked for licensed daycare facilities having excellent reputations with long waiting lists. That doesn't guarantee anything regarding the quality of care that will be provided by the people they hire that spend most of the time with the children. These people are different people than the administrators who create the programs offered. They may be excellent teachers with brilliant ideas but they are not the actual people who interact with the children.

July 2004

I rented an apartment to Emma, a single woman with a college degree in elementary education but left that field to work in a popular local daycare center. After about six months in my apartment she told me that she had been suspended for two weeks without pay while a "matter" involving a child was being investigated so she would not be able to pay rent on time that month. She assured me that it was a misunderstanding and that she would be reinstated. She was reinstated and the matter was soon forgotten about until it happened again eight months later. I really had a hard time believing that she could be guilty of possible child abuse but I do have to admit that the second allegation made me suspicious. Eventually I found out that Emma had two children of her own whom she did not have custody of.

In conversations with others who have worked in child care facilities they confirmed that this was the usual procedure when they expected child abuse. It is usually reported by another worker who saw something in person or on video surveillance and reported it. It is rarely reported by the parents who are unaware that their child may have been abused. It is rare that these suspensions ever lead to terminations because child abuse is not easy to prove. Most abusers do not have criminal or child abuse records which leaves them free to work in many childcare facilities for years

Late 1980's

In a neighboring county it was reported on the news that a four-month old baby was killed as a result of shaken baby syndrome. The news showed the home where the caregiver lived as being located in an upscale neighborhood. She was providing care for her own daughter and the brother of the baby that was killed, a total of three children. From her picture shown on the news, she looked like anyone that you would trust to provide excellent care to a child.

Not all of the details of crimes are reported because of the possibility of interfering with the police investigation. Years later, I met a relative of the child that had been killed. The caregiver and mother of the child had been good friends since childhood leaving the mother no reason to expect anything like this to happen and every reason to believe her child would be safe.

February 2011

In some cultures, there is no remorse or guilt by adults for the atrocities they commit against children. Consider the children in the Viet Nam war who approached American troops with dynamite strapped to their bodies who were blown up along with those they approached. This is an extreme case but nonetheless a case where it will be very difficult to convince the parents to get help. If they are in our country illegally or otherwise, they need to follow the laws that we have in place including the ones that protect children.

I rented an apartment to a couple whose family situation reeked of disrespect for each other but that was my interpretation which was different than theirs because of the different cultures we were raised in. The husband believed that his wife was his property and he had the right to control her and beat her. She would turn that abuse on her two young sons, ages two and four. While attempting to toilet train the younger child, she became violent and damaged a bathroom shower stall. She lied about it and said that she merely bumped into it when it looked like she took a sledge hammer to it. Various other items were broken in the apartment due to her problem with anger management. I had complaints from other tenants and neighbors. I tried to communicate to her that she was running a risk of losing her children to the foster care system. I was unable to get through to her because of the fact that she had been raised in a culture which does not define child abuse as we do in American culture. She had a third baby which pushed her over the edge. She beat both her kids badly enough requiring emergency medical care which resulted in all three children being placed in foster care. Both parents were required to go to counseling and parenting classes. In the year that they had no custody of their three children and did attend the classes, they made no progress. Eventually, the parents gave up all parenting rights and all three children were placed for adoption.

As drug use escalated, child protective services became more and more overloaded with complaint calls from citizens. I observed that those who worked for agencies dealing with the problems of abused children become more desensitized. The services that workers provided to children increased. Many of these children fell developmentally behind due to neglect. The abuse that many suffered required some form of therapy paid for by Medicaid.

One day I knocked on a door to have it quickly swing open by an eager small child. The mother briskly walked over to the child and kicked him across the room. It is bad enough that this abuse occurred in front of me but what was worse, is that two physical therapists who were in the apartment working with another child with questionable injuries also witnessed this. I asked the physical therapists what they were planning to do about what they had just witnessed and one of them replied that it was not their concern.

March 2012

Janelle was my first-floor tenant, a single mom of two elementary school aged boys. Her marriage ended when her husband went to prison for selling drugs. She was hard working never taking time off of work and mostly struggling to make ends meet. Her rent was a priority and always paid on time. She was not one to complain but one day she called me to tell me that there was a situation above her that needed to be addressed immediately. A family of a single mom and several daughters in their twenties had been living in the apartment above her for several months. Their drug habits had escalated out of control and when their mother left to visit relatives in another state for the weekend, the girls paid their drug debt by prostituting the oldest daughter, an eight-year old child out to their drug dealers. Janelle had called the police who told her to report it to Child Protective Services. That had been four days prior and Janelle was upset that no one had responded.

After a week went by and there was still no response from Child Protective Services, Janelle called me demanding that I take responsibility for what was going on in the apartment above her. In the past, whenever I called Child Protective Services, they were out immediately so I found it difficult to believe that a week had gone by while this horrific situation continued. She said she could not raise two impressionable young boys with this going on above her and would have to move. I promised her that I would call Child Protective Services as I had in the past for offenses far less than this.

I called Child Protective Services immediately and they said they would look into it. I argued with the woman on the phone that this needs to be addressed now, not looked into. She promised she would get to it. This went on for three days straight as I called every day. Janelle repeatedly called me begging me to do something about this as it was awful to listen to night after night. The last thing I wanted was to lose Janelle as a tenant. I was frustrated with Child Protective Services that they were not removing the child.

I was completely mystified when Janelle filed a discrimination suit against me with the department of affirmative action in the city. I looked at the paperwork in a true state of shock that I had received in the mail trying to make sense of it. The next day I ran into a neighbor on the block who worked for the Affirmative Action department in city hall. He had seen the discrimination complaint filed against me and told his boss he knew me well and would handle it with me personally. He had watched me rent apartments for years to whoever had the ability to pay. He had even observed a good relationship between me and the tenant that filed the complaint and believed that there was something more going on. That's when it hit me. Janelle had moved into my apartment nine months earlier due to code violations in her previous apartment. She had received funding through a program for her first month's rent and security deposit to move to my building since the code violations were considered an emergency situation. This program could only be used once a year and her year wasn't up.

Since Child Protective Services had not acted, Janelle felt she could not subject herself and her two boys to what was going on above her any longer. In filing a discrimination complaint against me was an attempt to create an emergency situation that would give her the security deposit and first month's rent needed to move. I told Marcus what I had just thought of and asked him if he could get me some help with Child Protective Services to have the eight-year old girl removed and placed in foster care. He shook his head and told me the Child Protective Services is overloaded with many complaints just like this one. They are doing the best they can to get to it but there are not enough investigators to investigate these allegations. Hiring the needed staff to address these complaints timely means additional funding which doesn't come without approval. This process can take months or the additional funding can be denied

Several weeks later, Child Protective Services came around to investigate and anyone who had anything to do with the apartment where the repeated abuse of the eight-year old had occurred left in the middle of the night. I did hear that they got one of the drug dealers who had participated in violating the child. The others were in the US illegally and it was assumed that they left the country quickly.

When I made promises to Janelle that the child would be rescued, I didn't realize that they can't possibly act as promptly as they did in the past. The difference is the number of undocumented children trafficked every day in this country. We don't begin to have anywhere near the manpower to investigate the claims we have presently. Many social workers did not sign up for a job where the dangers in situations such as children being trafficked are apparent. The most dangerous cases to be investigated seem to keep moving to the bottom of the pile.

Adults who were Abused as Children

Many children suffer abuse and sometimes without being discovered. They are abused physically and sexually by the people who are to care and protect them for their entire childhood until they leave home. They spend their entire adult life in therapy and on medication for a variety of mental illnesses due to childhood trauma. It is difficult for them to function as adults in society as they seem to continuously fail in both careers and relationships resulting in their dependency on our government to take care of them. For some others they are able to function by holding down jobs, supporting themselves and being responsible but perform below what they are truly capable of.

For many children that have grown up with the abuse taking place in the home in which they lived, it was often that someone had reported suspected abuse and investigations, sometimes many took place, but with nothing concrete being found, many continued to live and suffer that abuse until they were old enough to leave home.

It seems that once a child is in an abusive situation, it is almost impossible to escape. Sadly, it doesn't seem too different if the abuse is occurring by someone outside the home. This explains the adults who have come forward in record numbers with abuse allegations that occurred when they were children at the hands of clergymen, coaches, teachers, relatives or others who did not live with them.

Many pedophiles gain access to children by working with them in roles where they are trusted by everyone. This leaves victims completely confused, ashamed, or sometimes thinking they must somehow have some blame or maybe misunderstood the situation. No one has ever discussed with them that it may be possible that something like this can happen so when it does, they are completely unprepared to know how to handle it. When other victims come forward that removes all doubt for the victim of what actually did happen to them.

For parents who want to be guaranteed that their child won't become a victim, they cannot give anyone access to their child. Only parents can decide how much risk they are willing to take where their child is concerned. Some may think this is being too overprotective but for those who have been victimized it is a lifetime of recovery.

March 2019

I walked down the sidewalk in front of a building that I had owned for many years. Directly across the narrow street I was vaguely aware of a person who was walking at the same pace with his eyes on me. I turned to look at a handsome black man smiling at me. I smiled back and he said,

"You don't remember me do you Miss Marilyn?"

"Why don't you refresh my memory."

"I lived in that apartment building that you own many years ago"

"Which apartment?"

He pointed to a second-floor apartment with a large bay window. I did not recall anyone who looked like him ever living there.

"When did you live there?"

"twenty years ago, that's why you don't remember me, I was eight years old at the time. My mother was a crack whore working the streets and you called the police after one of my mother's boyfriends beat me because the TV was too loud."

It was a bad memory that I had pushed out of my mind for years, but now all of it came back to me. Neighbors had complained about him being left alone for hours in the apartment with no food. He had several older brothers who looked after him but they were never home. I remember being in the apartment the day he was removed by CPS. He was always sitting on the same dirty couch watching cartoons. His mother was in the bedroom with the door locked and his brothers were out. I sat down next to him and asked him if he was alright. He did not respond until I got up to leave. He ran over to me, hugging me tight and whispered, "please Miss Marilyn, don't go." As I hugged him back, he winced. I picked up his shirt to find welt marks across his back. Someone had beat him. I called the police and when they showed up, I told him that he needed to be removed from his mother's care.

"How is your mother?"

"She died of an overdose several years later."

"I'm so sorry,"

"Don't be, she made a lot of bad decisions in her life."

"How about your brothers?"

"Both in jail."

"How about yourself?"

"I'm working and I have a girlfriend, we have a son together."

"Please don't repeat that cycle of abuse, if you need help get it."

"I know that, I won't ever put my son through what I went through. I have seen you around and wanted to thank you for what you did for me. The problems at home were worse than you can imagine. Everyone thinks that foster care is really bad but I don't think I would be alive if it weren't for you calling the cops that day. Can I give you a hug?"

"You sure can."

12

DISABILITY

The source of income for those people either in our country illegally or migrating here from mostly New York and New Jersey was disability income. For many, a doctor had signed them up as having a mental disability or an addiction. In 1986 when I first started managing rental property, I did not have one tenant who collected disability income. It was well known that it was almost impossible to qualify for. In 1988 a couple applied for an apartment that I had advertised for rent. On the standard application form, I noticed that she had a job paying minimum wage, and he had no job and no income. He said that he was looking for a job in construction which was the type of work that he did before he was injured in an auto accident. He had not worked in a year due to the accident, and I was doubtful from looking at him that he would ever work again. He had back injuries in addition to a leg injury causing him trouble walking. He had spent a lot of time treating with doctors and in physical therapy. He had no choice but to find a job in construction (he was not trained to do anything else) as he had been turned down twice for disability income by the state.

I rented the apartment to them and hoped for the best. They did not have the expense of a car so it was possible for the two of them to live on minimum wage but it wasn't going to be easy. I never counted on him being able to go back to work and supplement their income. It was very obvious looking at him that just wasn't possible because of the injuries he had sustained in the accident.

They were ideal tenants always paying the rent on time in cash and would call me a few days before it was due to pick it up. After they had been there about six months, he called on a Monday to ask if I could come by sometime that day to pick up his rent. I knew the other tenants would have their rent on Wednesday so I asked if I could come by Wednesday when I would pick up all three apartments. He told me that I could come by Wednesday evening as he was starting a job on Wednesday and had a cash advance from his new employer. I asked what type of work it was and he told me hanging siding. I knew that this job would not last as he would not be able to do that type of work. It would be very risky for him to do that type of work with the injuries he already had causing any employer more liability than what they would be willing to take on.

On Tuesday, he committed suicide by sticking the barrel of a miniature cannon commonly used at high school football games in his mouth and blew his head off. They had constantly fought over money and his lack of contribution. She nagged him about getting a job which he was unable to do. She felt that if he didn't qualify for disability by the state, he could certainly get a job and contribute to their expenses. His disability made him dependent on her for a lot of help with everyday tasks such as bathing and dressing which made her feel as though she were taking care of a child.

The other tenants claimed that his girlfriend had threatened to leave if he didn't help with expenses. In desperation, he called a friend who hired him and gave him an advance on pay. He knew that he could not work one day so he committed suicide. He left a suicide note stating the rent money meant for me was in his pocket. I ended up in a dispute with the girlfriend who said she needed that money to pay funeral expenses and the contractor who said that it should be refunded to him since it was an advance that he had never worked for. I don't recall who the money went to but it didn't go to me. The damage he caused by the suicide was $8500 and I had a $250 insurance deductible which I paid out of pocket. My insurance company covered the balance of $8250. I was also out of rental income for three months while the apartment was cleaned up.

It was common during that time period to see Vietnam Vets living in the streets because of injuries they sustained in the war leaving them unable to work and being determined to be ineligible for disability benefits. I had people applying for apartments in wheelchairs who were confident that they would be approved for disability income but none of them were.

This all changed after unemployment was extended several times after the market crash. Between 2005 and 2007 due to the housing boom everyone was employed. I could not meet the demand of rental units for low income wage earners and every applicant was a good one. Not one was unemployed or disabled. At the time,

I had twenty-five units that paid every month and no evictions. The only people who were unemployed were hopelessly addicted to drugs.

In 2009 when the housing market crashed about 80% of these people were laid off. It still wasn't a problem though because of their eligibility for unemployment. When that ran out, an extension was granted and then another extension after that. I saw nothing but a steady decline in the housing market and knew that the economy was not getting better any time soon. I also knew that the extensions had to end eventually. What would happen when all of the extensions ended? I imagined that we would see overcrowded shelters and people living in the street as they would have no ability to pay rent.

What I saw in my rental units was that eventually the extensions did run out and the employment office told them to apply for disability. Every one of those unemployed people applied for disability benefits and they were all granted. Falling off the unemployment charts gave the impression that we had a much lower unemployment rate when in reality, if we combined both unemployment and disability recipients that were granted those disability benefits after their unemployment ran out, the numbers would have been staggering. It was the highest unemployment that I had ever seen among my tenants in thirty years of property management. If all of these people were working steadily for years, how did they all become disabled in the same year? They were not sick and not injured in an accident or a war. With the number of manufacturing jobs that had left the area as well as business closures due to the housing crisis, there was no choice but to put everyone on disability after that.

When prospective tenants applied for an apartment, I had an application that they filled out and would later be attached to their lease. One of the questions asked what their source of income was. It was shocking to see how these applicants went from 95% being employed to 95% being on disability income. For most I could not outwardly see what their disability was. One young man of about twenty years old told me that he collected $750 per month for being forgetful. I asked him to explain that a little further, and he told me that if he were going grocery shopping there were items that he would always forget by the time he got there. This person could be put to work at a manufacturing job that is repetitive where he doesn't have to remember multiple items. Many of the applicants told me that they collected disability for being "a little depressed." Some were disabled for being overweight and many were disabled for prior alcohol and drug abuse. While hearing these stories I could never forget the tenant who committed suicide for being unable to work. A man who had spent thirty years working and paying into the social security system as well as doing several tours of duty in Viet Nam, becomes disabled in an accident and is turned down for disability when he visibly can't walk. How is this right or just to turn him down but a young person who is a little "forgetful" is receiving disability benefits? The disability benefits granted after 2009 were more of an extension of unemployment than a true disability.

A tenant of mine had gotten a real estate license and had been questioned about extra income from the social security office. She was scared that if she got caught, she would lose all of her disability income so she told them she had gotten a real estate license. Her benefit was reduced. The problem with this is that our citizens who collect nothing are working very hard and paying taxes into social security to compete with people who do not contribute and are collecting what we put into the social security system. They are then taking business and our jobs away from us.

I saw a lot of people disabled due to prior drug abuse. Drugs alter people's minds permanently sometimes so that they are never able to function again in their lifetime in society and become labeled as being mentally ill. After the market crash selling drugs was a way for some people to support themselves and lack of enforcement at our borders meant that it became an easy business. The drug epidemic that our country has faced in recent years have ruined many families as well as lives and has placed a great financial burden on our country not only in disability payments but also treatment that is covered under Medicaid. People who have become casualties are so monumental that it is downright shocking. Treatment centers, shelters, and nursing homes are always full leaving many living on the streets.

Many women apply for apartments over fifty years old that are disabled and collecting disability income mostly due to substance abuse. When I would ask about their disability, they said that they had a stroke some as young as forty-five years old. The stroke had left them incontinent, overweight, high blood pressure and having basically all of the characteristics of someone at the end of their life expectancy. Many went back and forth from my apartment to a nursing home paid for by Medicaid. They desperately wanted to live independently but were unable to do so and required assistance. It was important for me to know about their disability so that I could be assured that I was renting them an apartment that would be appropriate. I would later find out that they were drug addicts and that the stroke they had was a result of years of drug addiction. The other symptoms such as incontinence were a symptom of the stroke. They had spent years in treatment centers to only continue to regularly relapse. The only thing that was left was to place them in a nursing home under Medicaid where they were given their meds in addition to Methadone.

The cycle of going back and forth from an apartment to a nursing home was routine for one of my tenants that lasted several years until she finally moved in with a family member. She had once been a wife and a mother living in the suburbs before drugs stole her life. She was too embarrassed to be honest with me and tell me how it all got started. Many people like her had children who wanted nothing to do with a parent with an addiction problem so their parents became dependent on the state for care. She overdosed and ended up in a hospital and then went onto a nursing home for nine months to rehabilitate. When she came back there was always a drug dealer nearby to supply her habit.

Many of these people had caseworkers but needed and required more care than that. Drug abuse had caused them to become dysfunctional requiring help in areas of life that we all take for granted. They needed help in making doctor's appointments, calling the social security office when changes occurred in their benefits mostly through using state facilities, obtaining prescriptions and many other areas of their life. I would know they were a drug addict when they had no choice but to ask me to pick up their prescriptions and I picked up Methadone. Or they would ask for help with calling for a prescription and would give me the prescription list. I would notice again that Methadone was on the list. I saw too many people like this that our government has spent thousands of dollars on treating drug abuse which will last this person's entire lifetime.

It appears that many disability policies became looser with the downtown of the economy causing us to go from one extreme to the other. Many of the policymakers have made these policies without a big picture in mind. In other words, how do some of these policies affect the rest of the population? It is imperative that this is considered because after all, the segment of the population that funds disability through the social security they contribute to through the regular payments they make may become disabled themselves because of certain policies that are put in place.

Emotional Support Animals

Thirty-five years ago, I allowed tenants to have a dog in return for fifty dollars more a month. I lost money on every single tenant as carpets had to be replaced as well as doors that had been heavily scratched. The most responsible owners were not always home to walk a dog and did not work close enough to take the dog out on their lunch break. Sometimes they were required to work overtime leaving the dog alone in the apartment beyond the amount of time that would be reasonable.

Certain laws have been enacted regarding emotional support animals. I have been told by a real estate office renting property for me out of state, that a person protected under FHA and ACAA laws supersedes a person having a serious medical condition. This forced me to rent a property to a tenant who informed the realtor after signing a lease with a no pet policy that he was getting an emotional support dog. Both my husband and I are allergic to dogs causing us respiratory problems which need to be treated by a doctor. The fact that an animal had been occupying the property now has to be disclosed to future tenants causing the property to become unavailable to others who have allergies to animals. There is no requirement other than a therapist signing paperwork that the patient has a need for an emotional support dog. That encourages deceitful people to have a doctor sign a note for them saying that they need an emotional support animal. Many people who have true disabilities in the form of mental illness and other emotional problems do not provide good homes for pets. Instead of them providing emotional support, many times the pet becomes a scapegoat and suffers abuse and eventually abandonment by the owner.

13

MENTAL ILLNESS

With a vast majority of people collecting disability benefits due to mental illness, we have lost sight of what a true disabling case of mental illness really is. Mental illness includes depression, bipolar disorder, schizophrenia as well as mental illnesses with no specific identification. Most people with mental illness can be treated with medication having results that are successful enough to give them the ability to lead a relatively normal life including being employed. The more serious cases are very crippling causing those people to be unable to function well enough to be successful in relationships or employment. We often hear of the most violent cases in the media however, most are not violent. Not every mentally ill person is confined to a mental institution or a psychiatric ward but live on their own on disability income from the state and services are provided to them through a caseworker. The amount of time that they get with a case worker depends on a mental evaluation.

Whenever I had a difficult tenant, I would run through a checklist that I had compiled over the years and check off the symptoms that these tenants had pointing to various degrees of mental illness. This list helped me understand that this person had a problem that would eventually affect the other tenants in the building causing me to lose all other tenants if I didn't find help. A caseworker is trained in mental illness to act on their behalf which is very helpful but many still fall through the cracks and don't get the level of service that they need. They generally have poor relationships with people including their families which make it impossible to get help from them. Because of the difficulty they have in relationships, it is not always possible for them to be employed.

I have profiled five mentally ill people below that I have dealt with that are true disabling cases for collecting disability for their mental illness.

Alice

Alice's case worker called me on an ad I had placed in the classified advertising section of the newspaper for an apartment for rent. Alice was a woman in her fifties who had recently lost her husband due to a drug overdose and had been evicted from her apartment for hoarding. She had been living in a shelter and was soon to be evicted as her allowable time in the shelter was about to expire. She spent her days going to support groups for depression and wandering around the city pulling a shopping cart. Other days she spent hours sleeping caused by the various medications she took evidenced by the empty medicine bottles she hoarded.

On the days that I collected rent she would not invite me into the apartment so would I wait outside her door as the minutes ticked by while she looked for her checkbook in the hoard. She was one of the few tenants I took a check from knowing that a case worker was monitoring her finances. As much as she tried to hide the mess by opening up the door just a crack, it was still enough for me to see the dishes piled up in the sink and then on the stove as she ran out of space. I always told her she had to clean up and she always said she was working on it.

One year as spring approached there was a faint bad smell coming from her apartment. I was going to schedule a maintenance check but then got sidetracked when I had a fire in the four-unit building, I owned next door that also spread to the top floor of the three-unit apartment building where Alice lived. That apartment had been steadily rented for thirty years that I had owned it and I decided that in addition to cleaning up the smoke damage I would also remodel the kitchen and bath while it was vacant. My plumber mentioned the bad smell in the hallway as spring turned to summer and the temperatures rose. That seemed very minor considering the fire damage I had in the two buildings. The other tenant below complained as roaches crawled through the ceiling at night. I did a maintenance check on Alice's apartment while she was out since she avoided me and would not let me enter the apartment. Trash was piled everywhere as well as numerous flyers that she had picked up in the street and brought home for no particular reason. The smell was so over powering that as I entered the bathroom, it looked like the toilet had become stopped up and the bathtub was then being used as a toilet which was also stopped up. There were three feet of used disposable adult diapers and clothing piled high. I grabbed a trash bag along with rubber gloves and cleaned out everything throwing it in garbage bags and tossing it out the window to a trash can below. I filled every trash can until I couldn't fill anymore. I called in a pest control company who bombed every month for the next six months. After the major clean up I did in Alice's apartment that day, she stayed home barricading herself in the apartment to ensure that I wouldn't come in and continue to clean up. I fought with her to get the plumber to come in and unclog the bathtub and toilet and then put her on a payment plan to pay the bill. I called her case worker to discuss various paragraphs in her lease that she was violating. Her case worker would try to catch up with her to help with correcting the violations only to be avoided

Meanwhile she was always in violation of two paragraphs of her lease agreement stating that she agreed to keep the apartment in the same repair and condition as when it was originally rented to her and that she agreed not to infringe upon the rights of other tenants. Members from Alice's church often checked in on her and if she stayed in her apartment for days on end, I would get phone calls from them asking me to check on her. Every so often Alice was hospitalized for mental illness and this cycle continued for years.

Her case worker was also unable to have the required meetings with her when Alice would shut herself off from the world so I would meet the caseworker and open the door for her. Alice would be sleeping for hours around the clock and when we would access the apartment, we would find her in her pajamas and sleepy no matter what time of day it was. She appeared to be very zombie like as the case worker tried to get her point across that she needed to take control of her life and correct the violations in this apartment before she loses it. She would say nothing and continue to stare at the floor. I remember bringing to the case worker's attention that Alice had a cockroach squashed on her back from sleeping. She made no motion to brush it off. The case worker asked her how she had bathed with her bathtub being unusable. She admitted to the caseworker that she hadn't bathed or showered in a year.

As the 2016 presidential election approached between Donald Trump and Hillary Clinton, she became an advocate for Hillary Clinton working at a call center making random phone calls in support of Hillary Clinton. This got her out of the apartment and she seemed a little less depressed. One day as she was leaving the building, she confronted me while on a maintenance check and accused me in an angry way of being a Trump supporter. She went on to tell me that Donald Trump was a threat to people like her dependent on government assistance and that if he were elected her disability checks would stop. We had seen an influx of people from out of town in our streets giving out inaccurate information to people like Alice. I tried to assure her that was false but this idea had been driven into her during her volunteer work leaving her feeling so threatened and believing that she had no other choice but to work at a telephone call center every day to convince people not to vote for Donald Trump.

While leaving the telephone call center Alice tripped and fell down the stairs breaking her shoulder. She ended up in a nursing home recuperating for three months where she found a whole new set of friends and activities. Her spirits seemed more upbeat when she got a roommate whose boyfriend would hang out most of the day and they would all laugh and joke together.

The tenant below Alice had moved out because of the roach problem that was very difficult to control due to Alice's hoarding. One evening while showing the apartment to a prospective tenant a church member came by to feed Alice's cat. He was surprised to see the condition of the apartment as he had gotten a different story. Alice had told people in her church group that the reason why her apartment was such a mess was that I refused to fix anything. This church member immediately saw the problem when he entered the apartment. He said that he knew she had problems with depression and remarked that he was glad that she found an outlet working for the Democratic Party even though he didn't share her political beliefs. The conversation turned around to the election. The church member told me that he had spent his life as a limo driver chauffeuring executives of local companies. During a charity dinner he chauffeured an executive who had met and talked with Ben Carson about his endorsement of Donald Trump. Ben Carson apparently had spoken to many people in and around Donald Trump's golf courses including people who worked for him before endorsing him.

During the election, many small business contractors who worked for me would be cautious about talking about the election. My small business provided housing to primarily low-income people and many dependent on government assistance. Many people interpreted that to mean that all government assistance and food stamps would be taken away from people who needed that instead of people leaving that behind because of gainful employment when jobs came back. The counselors and case workers whose employment was dependent on serving those people that I housed were not in favor of Donald Trump because of the fear of losing their jobs through budget cuts. If we did talk about the election, they all said the same thing about how many people they kept talking to that were telling a different story than the media.

Finally, Alice was released from the nursing home and came back to live at the apartment. I went over to collect rent and then my plan was to file for eviction. I knew that I could not go through another warm season as this would bring out roaches all over again and I couldn't keep losing good tenants. What I found was that Alice had brought the roommate and her boyfriend home to live with her. The apartment was immaculate as these two people worked very hard to clean it all up. I was in a state of shock and even though Alice was in violation of her lease under a different paragraph, the one that stated she could not move random people in, I was willing to overlook that violation for the time being. The boyfriend had been living in a homeless shelter and Alice's newfound friend, Rita, had been homeless and was not able to be placed in a shelter. Ever since the downturn of the economy, many people lost homes due to foreclosure or apartments due to eviction. If they didn't have a vehicle to live in, they needed help in being placed somewhere especially in the winter months. Many were being placed in nursing homes under Medicaid due to running out of space at the local shelters which is how Rita ended up as Alice's roommate in the nursing home.

During cleanup it became obvious that there was nothing of use in Alice's apartment. The couch was broken and couldn't be sat on and there was not enough closet space to store canned goods. When a new couch was purchased and a kitchen shelving unit, this left Alice short on paying her rent. Her account was overdrawn and I was told at the bank that funds were insufficient to pay her rent. I called her case worker and she met with Alice and Rita to tell them that they had a budget in place and Alice could not afford anything extra.

Rita's boyfriend was stealing money off of Rita and Alice's Access cards and was thrown out. Immediately, Rita found another boyfriend, Lester, and he moved in. There seemed to be conflict between Rita and Alice after Lester moved in so Lester and Rita decided to rent the apartment below when that became available.

Within three days of Rita and Lester moving to the apartment below, Rita kicked Lester out and Alice took him in. This caused a lot of commotion because Rita wanted him in the street and out of the building. He was eventually placed in a homeless shelter and things settled down although there was still tension between Alice and Rita. Both told me various negative things about the other on different occasions.

On the first of the month I went into Rita's apartment which was always immaculate. When I sat on the couch across from her while I looked for her receipt in my receipt book, she said to me, "if I were you, I wouldn't sit there." "why not?" I asked. "Alice came in the other day and sat there and when she got up to leave, I noticed that she had wet her pants." I laughed believing that it was another negative thing being said that wasn't necessarily true.

I then went to Alice's apartment and found it a total mess with garbage piled up as well as dishes piled in the sink. I could see that the apartment was quickly going back to the previous condition before Rita had cleaned it up. Alice sat on the new couch which was already dirty staring at the floor. A plastic shelving unit had been knocked over spilling its contents every in the path of anyone that would walk from the kitchen to the living room.

"What's wrong", I asked

"I'm depressed,

"What happened?"

Alice continued to stare at the floor and not move.

"I'm here to collect rent, where is your checkbook." She shrugged and continued to stare at the floor. I looked around and started to move piles of papers on the table. She reached in back of her under a pile of junk on the couch and came up with the rent check which was filled out incorrectly.

"I can't take this to the bank, they won't take it, do you have another check."

She continued to stare at the floor. Again, I started going through junk and she pulled her book of checks from another pile of junk. I filled out a check correctly and had her sign it.

For several days I wondered if she would do something like take her own life. It bothered me and I decided to go back and check on her. She wouldn't answer the door so I used my key and went in. There was a paragraph in my leases that stated that I could enter the apartment for emergencies at any time and I considered this an emergency.

I found Alice in the exact same spot on the couch staring at the floor. The shelf was still tipped over blocking the pathway from the kitchen to the living room.

"Alice, have you moved from this couch since I saw you in the last couple of days." I asked. She continued to stare at the floor.

"You can't just sit here for days on end like this"

"Alice, have you even moved off this couch to sleep in your own bed in your bedroom?" I asked.

With that question she looked at me and said,

"I can't sleep in my bed because when Rita lived here, she slept in my bed and she used to wet the bed every night."

"Oh, come on," I said.

"If you don't believe me go check it out for yourself.

I had no desire to walk around the apartment any more than I had to. I called the caseworker and reported what I had seen over the last couple of days and what I had just left. She told me that she had tried to contact Alice all week because she had missed appointments and was unable to reach her. She had gone to the apartment and knocked but Alice would not open the door. The caseworker was out of town that day and it was a Friday but told me that she would meet me first thing on Monday morning. I wondered if this situation could really wait until Monday but I guessed it would have to.

At 8:30am on Monday morning the caseworker and I stood at Alice's door and knocked and there was no answer. I put my key in the lock and turned the knob and walked in. Alice was still sitting in the same spot on the couch. The stench was overpowering.

We both entered the living room stepping over the shelf and its contents that was still exactly as I had left it the week before. The case worker pulled out an Ipad and pulled up her information on Alice. I had come in with a box of garbage bags and filled them up and threw them out the window to the trash cans below.

The caseworker was asking her if she had taken her meds and she didn't know. She then asked where they were and she didn't know. We went through the piles of junk and all we came up with were empty bottles. The caseworker got authorization to talk with her therapist. While looking for the meds through piles, I found stacks of psychiatric reports which I handed to the caseworker. She noted that they were Lester's reports and not Alice's so I threw them in a trash bag with a lot of other junk.

The caseworker and I had met in Alice's apartment about a half a dozen or so times like this and the meeting always went the same way. I listened to the same conversation again that day.

"Alice, we have a problem here, you are about to be evicted from your apartment for the condition that this apartment is in which is attracting bugs and costing your landlord $150 a monthly to exterminate. What do you think we should do about this problem"?

No response

"Alice, what plan do you have to correct this problem?"

No response

"Alice, do you realize the seriousness of what you are faced with here?"

No response

"Alice, we are going to need to start with you answering my questions, I can't help until we can do that?"

No response

"Alice, we are going to need to start by coming up with a plan of cleaning every day." You need to start today, as a matter of fact right now with getting off the couch and getting a trash bag and throwing things out"
No response

I bent down to pick up the shelf between the kitchen and the living room. As I bent down, the smell of urine almost knocked me over. I looked up from the floor and that's when I saw that Alice was sitting on a hospital pad that you would use for an incontinent patient. She had used this repeatedly as a toilet instead of getting up to use the bathroom.

The caseworker had not noticed as she was busy making notes on her ipad.

"Alice, what will happen if you get evicted, where will you go and what will you do?"

"I'll just get another apartment".

"With what money"?

"With state funding, just like I got when I rented this apartment. They will pay my first month's rent and security deposit just like before."

"That particular program has no more money in it, it is completely dried up. There is no money in your checking account and we are struggling to pay your heating bills. How are you going to come up with a first month's rent and security deposit?"

No Response

"And I'll tell you right now, all the shelters in the city are full, as I have tried to get someone shelter last week to be turned away, there is no room so that isn't an option either"

"I won't go to a shelter I refuse to be sexually assaulted there."

I looked up and said, "Oh I'm sure that you don't need to worry about that"

"I would rather live in the street than in a shelter"

"Today is an unseasonably warm day but we also have to remember that it is January. There are many cold days ahead before spring. You can't live in the street at this time of year. The best option is to clean up this apartment and hope that your landlord allows you to stay."

All of a sudden Alice jumped off the couch and shouted at me "don't you throw my valuable things out."

That's when the caseworker noticed the hospital pad and the back of Alice's pants with dark stains.

"Alice, have you wet your pants."

No response

"Alice, go change those wet pants immediately, and when you come back out don't sit down, we are going to start cleaning up when you get back."

When she left the room, I grabbed the hospital pad and threw it in a trash bag. I looked at the new couch that wasn't even six weeks old and that was urine soaked as well. The cat came over and tried to use the litter box that was next to the couch. It had not been changed for a long time and the cat could not use it. When Alice came back the counseling conversation continued.

"Alice, the cat is trying to use the litter box and there is nowhere for her to go. Have you fed the cat or given her water?"

"Yes, can't you see that for yourself?"

"No, I don't see a food bowl or a water bowl. "

"It's under the papers over there."

I picked up a large pile of papers to find an empty completely dry bowl.

"Is that the cat's water bowl?"

"Why are you asking me such stupid questions, you know that's the cat's water bowl?"

"When was the last time it had water in it?"

"It has plenty of water in it, can't you see that for yourself. Stop asking me all of these questions, I'm not answering any more of them."

"Alice, get the cat litter scooper and a trash bag and clean the cat's litter now or the cat will have to go to an animal shelter, because her needs are not being met here."

"You can't do that you are violating my rights."

"Please change the litter now, so that she can stay here, and when you are done changing the litter, please feed your cat and get her a bowl of water."

After she did all of that, the caseworker told her that she would be back in two days to check the apartment.

"Your landlord has done a lot already while we have been here today which she doesn't have to do at all. She has been very generous but it is now time for you to take responsibility for the rest."

The caseworker and I left the apartment together and walked down the dark hallway and a flight of steps and out into a bright balmy January morning. We both breathed the outside fresh air in an attempt to quickly forget the stench that we had just come from.

We stood in front of the building in silence and still reeling from the situation. We had been through this several times before with Alice.

I said, "I think we can both agree that Alice needs to be institutionalized."

"The state will never pay for that"

"I'm no authority of what the mentally ill qualifies for but I have this feeling that she is falling through the cracks. This level of care that she does receive from the state seems to be inadequate."

"I have a large caseload of people like this I handle. I can make recommendations but her assessment does not indicate that she needs any more care than what she is already receiving."

I already knew that as I had seen many cases of mental illness over the years. We don't provide the help that is needed for people who are our own citizens and we want to welcome more people that can't provide for themselves. I saw firsthand our generosity of supporting people who have done nothing for our country, while I have stepped over our veterans sleeping in the street or downtown on park benches because there was no room in shelters for them. Meanwhile I also saw firsthand through property management that our government provided housing vouchers, food stamps, free utilities, free education, and free healthcare to illegal immigrants who have never paid one dime of taxes while they allow an American citizen like Alice to sit in her own waste.

What is mental illness? That is a complicated question to answer. After dealing with a handful of people early on I thought I knew the answer. Then I would deal with another mentally ill person that would leave me asking more questions about mental illness and realizing that I didn't have all of the answers.

For many people it was long term drug abuse or occasional use that had bad effects many years later. Their brains were so fried, they were unable to budget money without help from a counselor, unable to remember to pay bills resulting in utilities being shut off, forgetting appointments, and not having the ability to do even the simplest job meaning unemployment which eventually resulted in being placed on permanent disability. For some others having mental illness meant that they have suffered long term physical, emotional or sexual abuse when they were children. Many turned to drugs as a way of self-medicating and coping with a lot of bad memories. Some had faced trauma such as fighting in wars causing post-traumatic stress syndrome.

Alice's mental state grew progressively worse over the seven years or so that she rented an apartment from me. By the time she was fifty-five years old she was placed in a nursing home funded by Medicaid.

Jason

Jason was a case of a mentally ill person who grew up in a home in a tight knit suburban neighborhood where everyone knew everyone else and looked out for each other. He had the model family of two parents who were never unemployed and provided a good living for him and his two older sisters. Jason did well in high school academically and was popular with other model students. He had never been in any trouble and was considered by everyone who knew him to be a great guy who would do great things in his adult life. After high school, Jason was accepted at a college about an hour away from his hometown where he would study engineering. He adapted to college life very quickly and continued to do as well as he did in high school. He made a whole new set of friends and joined a fraternity.

During his fraternity days, he had experimented with drugs, one of them being LSD. He dated in college but did not form any serious relationships as he was very career oriented and wanted to get established there first. Upon graduation, he was immediately offered full time employment at a company between Reading and Philadelphia. He did very well at work being quickly promoted with more responsibility within a year. He met a young woman his age at work and they became involved in a relationship. Everything was going very well for Jason both at work and financially.

Within two years of dating Jason and Kristen were married. They were both steadily employed with no chance of a layoff as they were both high achieving. They had saved 25% for a down payment in addition to closing costs. They were extremely easy to work with as they were both very smart, made a great home buying decision and had no concerns or anxiety as many young homebuyers do. Their goal was to work a few more years and pay down principle before starting a family.

I had kept in touch with them fairly regularly with an occasional holiday card and phone call. Two years passed and there was no mention of moving or starting a family. My conversations were very pleasant with them and I did not sense from those conversations that anything was wrong.

Eight years later I got a call from Kristen to list their home for sale, they were getting divorced. Jason was mentally disabled and had been institutionalized several times during their marriage. She hoped that he would recover and they could go on to live a normal life but that never happened. Living with him had become difficult as described by Kristen and something she just didn't want to live with any longer. She longed to have a family but knew that Jason could not participate as a father because of the mental illness he suffered. It was the last person that I would have ever thought that something like this would happen to. There had been no history of anything like this in his family.

Kristen described this as being very subtle and not really noticeable by her at first. It started with problems at work with coworkers but around the time those problems started new people had been hired and Kristen assumed there were personality conflicts. His stellar reviews at work over the years turned the other way. Jason became unable to function in simple tasks that he had done around the house. This was very frustrating to Kristen as more and more responsibility was piled on her as he became more incapable. Jason developed sleeping and eating disorders causing weight gain which in turn caused high blood pressure, high cholesterol, heart palpitations and dizziness. They went to marriage counseling where it was pointed out to them that Jason may have mental problems and should be evaluated. He was put on different medications that didn't seem to help and brought on other symptoms. Eventually, he went out on permanent disability.

No one really knew what the cause of all of this behavior was, however according to Kristen, Jason still kept in touch with one of his fraternity brothers who had also experimented with LSD and had all of the same problems. Maybe this was the connection to Jason's problems and maybe it was just a coincidence. The sad part of this is that if LSD was the cause, it ruined his life with just a handful of times experimenting and not until many years later. At the time of their divorce, Jason was no longer capable of living on his own. If he wasn't in a mental institution, he was living in a skilled nursing facility recuperating or home with his parents.

Kenny

Kenny had been a very average kid growing up in an average suburban neighborhood. He was the younger of two boys and had a reasonably good childhood with two loving and attentive parents. In high school he began to experience mood swings with periods of deep depression so crippling that he was unable to get out of bed some mornings to go to school. Immediately, his parents sought medical attention for him and he was diagnosed with bipolar disorder. They were able to put him on medication and everything went quickly back to normal.

After graduating from high school, Kenny was able to find a job in the office at the steel factory where his father and grandfather had both worked. He worked there steadily, living at home and saving money. In his mid-twenties he was anxious to leave his parent's home and start a life of his own. He had worked full time for seven years and had saved 30% down and closing costs that would buy a new construction home in a desirable location. Shortly after moving into the home he met a girl his age and she moved into his home with him. Within a year they became engaged and started to plan a wedding. They were entering their late twenties and she was anxious to start a family and quit working to stay at home and be a full-time mother.

I was very surprised when I got a call from Kenny three years later to come list the home because he was on permanent disability from work and was not sure if he would ever be able to work again.

The wedding was several months away when Kenny started experiencing all of the symptoms of bipolar disorder that he had experienced ten years before. He had never stopped taking his medication in all of that time but somehow the medication stopped working. Doctors tried other medications but they were all unsuccessful. Kenny's fiancé broke the engagement and went on to marry someone else.

Kenny did not blame her for leaving him as he said no one could ever live with anyone who had bipolar disorder that was left uncontrolled. He had been up front with her about his condition, but he explained no one really knows what they are getting into until they actually have to live with someone who has this condition. The medication beautifully masked the disorder which was not really a true picture of what this person was really like. In his case, there was no trace of the problem at all with the medication that he was on for ten years. They eventually were able to somewhat control his bipolar disorder with other medications but none others had the result that the first medication had.

Because of his mental unstableness, he was moving back home with his parents. His house quickly sold and I surmised that as bad as his condition was during that sale, it was doubtful that his life would ever be the same allowing him to become a buyer for a home again.

For those that had mental illness, I would not attempt to rent an apartment to them without a caseworker who I could communicate with if needed. Many fell out of programs or left institutions and attempted to live on their own.

Nelda

Nelda had once lived in a nice home in the suburbs before her husband left her and filed for divorce. She was not working at the time of her divorce but did get a job and tried to keep the house. The house that she fought to keep was unaffordable on her income and eventually she found herself in foreclosure. On the day that she was forced to move from the house, she was unable to find alternative housing including emergency shelters as it was wintertime and they were all full. She was placed in a nursing home paid for by Medicaid even though she was only fifty years old as a temporary housing situation. She became severely depressed and suicidal and was admitted to a psychiatric hospital. It was determined by a doctor that she was unable to work and went on disability. Eventually she was released from the mental institution and was back at another nursing home funded by Medicaid where she lived for two years. She left the nursing home and was placed in one of my rental units through an agency. She did not qualify for a case worker so I believed at the time she would not be too difficult to handle.

Nelda spent her days harassing other tenants for cigarettes, money, meals, pills, drugs, rides to the store, and creating general chaos in the building. When her doctor refused to fill prescriptions for her, she would call an ambulance to go to the hospital and threaten suicide if they didn't fill her up. It wasn't long before every tenant in the building moved out and she stopped paying rent when she couldn't manage her disability income. When I filled the other units, the new tenants told me why my other tenants refused to stay. What I was aware of with Nelda was just the tip of the iceberg. Her mental problems ran much deeper than what I would have ever imagined.

I called an agency for help in getting her back into a state funded nursing facility. She was definitely one of those people who fell through the cracks. A caseworker checking in on her while living alone was not an adequate arrangement. She left behind boxes of medical records indicating a long history of psychiatric problems.

Some people are a danger to society if they are not on medication. We have controlled this by assigning them a caseworker who can make sure they are constantly monitored to be able to live in society.

When they stop taking medication, there will be behavior changes that can put others at risk. A case worker is trained to identify that during their regular visits and will get them back on track.

During the pandemic mental health services operated with a limited staff. Many were not getting their regular appointments so many of their needs were not being met. When mentally ill people do not get the help they need, their mental condition gets worse. During the pandemic, I called mental health services on eight people. Mental health was able to intervene on all of the cases except for one.

Steve

Steve, single with no children had lived in my apartment for several years. He was employed full time never causing any problems. In February, he had gone into the hospital for surgery. On the day he was discharged, the hospital shuttle service dropped him off at home where he took off the front door of his apartment while the keys laid beside it and went to bed. That morning when I pulled up in front of the building, the police were out front talking to a neighbor whose home had been burglarized during the night while he slept. Several tenants in my building called to tell me that Steve's door was taken off the hinges which lead me to believe that the same people had burglarized him.

While speaking to my handyman that day I asked him to make reinstalling Steve's door a priority and to look around and see if it looked like anything had been stolen. I assumed that Steve was still in the hospital since I had not heard from him. As he walked through the apartment checking, Steve came out of the bedroom and demanded to know why he was in his apartment. He confronted me with the same questions about why the handyman was in his apartment and I apologized and explained the situation. He didn't seem to remember taking the door off the hinges. This behavior was out of the ordinary but I guessed that it had something to do with side effects from the medication he was given due to his surgery and he would be back to normal in a few days. Steve's behavior did not change but got worse.

I began getting some unusual text messages from Steve about people that had entered his apartment and were shooting at him. He hung notes in his windows warning people about spying on him. I called mental health services the next day asking them for help for Steve. A few days later, according to several witnesses, Steve pulled a knife and was threatening people. They called the police and he locked himself away in his apartment and refused to answer the knock on the door by the police. The police called me to get verification of Steve's full name for a citation that they were hanging on his door so that the court system could deal with it. Steve was a white man but with everything that had gone on in the death of George Floyd, the police were no longer making arrests or confronting people breaking the law. I got calls from other tenants in the building describing behavior issues which were very out of the ordinary for Steve. We were all very concerned and believing that I could reason with him, I knocked on his door. Steve refused to answer but one day I saw him walking into the building and up the stairs and followed him. As he got to the top of the stairs and I stood at the bottom I called out his name and he turned to look at me.

"Steve, what seems to be the problem," I asked.

"I'm sick and tired of everyone that is against me and out to get me." He said.

We were still a staircase apart when he pulled out a long rod from behind his back. I asked him what it was.

"It's a weapon and I'm using it on everyone who gets in my way." He said.

"Put the weapon down," I said

It folded and he put it away in some pocket he had behind him.

"I have maintenance work that needs to be done in this building and I can't get anyone to come in here and do this work after the knife incident with the police." I said.

"I need to protect myself against everyone who is threatening me in any way." He said.

"Whose threatening you," I asked.

"Your workers are looking in my windows." He said

"I will talk to my workers and tell them not to have any communication with you and I expect you to have no communication with them."

The next day I called mental health and told them what had happened. That's when I learned that my first complaint was filed to the bottom of the pile when they told me they could not address this situation without police protection. Steve stopped paying rent because he believed that his apartment had become unsafe and I was not doing anything about it. I went down to the police department and spoke with them about the situation and they told me to evict him. As I walked into the district court with my paperwork and check to pay for a legal eviction, the clerk informed me that the governor had just shut down the court system. I could not get this person out without a legal eviction which our governor had made impossible. In this case, there was no mental health, no police protection, and no court system. They have disabled law and order leaving the door open to potential catastrophes and completely failing Steve. This is very sad because there are many people like him that are living among us and without the help that they need, they end up jobless and then homeless and a danger to society.

I found that many who were diagnosed as being mentally ill landed in low income housing but were not necessarily raised there such as the five examples I have outlined. Many grew up in families who had the resources to get help in the form of counseling that may have gone on for years. For the group that seemed to fit into emotional disorders there seemed to be no magic pill or answer to give them the ability to function in society and become independent. Eventually counseling services certified them as disabled and they are then evaluated by the state to determine what services they need.

14

HEALTHCARE

Healthcare Yesterday

When I was growing up in the 1960's and 1970's healthcare was very simple. Everyone had healthcare provided for them as a benefit through their employer and everyone was employed. There were two types of healthcare insurance, plans with deductibles and copays and plans with no deductibles and no copays. You could usually tell which family had which plan by how they treated healthcare.

For my parents, it was a plan with deductibles and copays. They would not seek medical care unless it was necessary treating much of our family's ailments with over the counter medications. For those families with father's who worked as laborers represented by unions, they had plans with no deductibles and no copays.

The families with no deductibles and no copays would skip the over the counter medications and call the doctor for any minor ailment. The doctor knowing the ailment was minor and one that he didn't have to see them for would call in an antibiotic. He would charge their insurance for an office visit which the patient would not question because it was fully covered by their healthcare insurance. This was an easy practice with those patients who carried no deductible and no copay plans as they were not aware that the doctor was charging for an office visit when there was no office visit. For most ailments an antibiotic is not needed, but over the counter medication, drinking plenty of water and getting extra rest is sufficient. Prescribing an antibiotic indicates that the patient needs medical care beyond over the counter medications which would also indicate that the patient needs to be seen. Insurance companies would assume that the patient was seen before the doctor would prescribe any medications. For the patient, his medical care is free, not needing to spend any money on over the counter medications. This was the beginning of fraud and abuse of healthcare. Looking at the big picture, if a large number of patients handle their healthcare in this way insurance premiums eventually would have to increase to cover the extra cost that is incurred which is exactly what happened.

There are times when we have all had unexpected medical problems that come up that are considered emergencies. Our primary physician would advise us to visit an emergency room where we would be seen immediately as emergencies are rare. When I was a child, we were visiting my grandmother over the summer when I ran a high fever. My parents took me to the emergency room at the hospital where my grandmother lived. There were true emergencies there that day. A man had been in a motor cycle accident and broke his leg. A woman had slipped and fallen down a hill and kept rolling until her head hit a tree and she was in a coma. A woman brought her husband in who was having chest pain and he was immediately seen.

In the early 1980's I was part of a three-car collision involving a drunk driver. Everyone involved were taken to the emergency room and checked out for injuries. The whole procedure took about twenty minutes from the time we checked in, to the time we checked out. Also, during the 1980's I suffered a severe migraine headache over a weekend and went to an emergency room for treatment where I was seen immediately. It was a relief just knowing that even though the doctor's office was closed, treatment was still available.

In the early to mid-1980's I had two hospital stays for childbirth. For the first delivery I had excellent healthcare insurance fully paid for by my employer as a benefit. I was leaving work and would then go under my husband's plan. My husband's plan which he contributed to had deductibles. My plan through my employer had no deductibles so of course my plan was the better plan. My concern was that my baby was due in the middle of the month and my plan ended at the end of that month since I was not returning to work. My doctor assured me that they would induce labor before my plan ended. When I had twins, I was covered under my husband's plan. I had deductibles for each twin and myself, a lot of money to pay out of pocket for young people trying to raise a family on one income. During both of my hospital stays I felt like I got excellent care. I believe that this was the result of several things. The hospital was adequately staffed, the staff genuinely enjoyed their jobs, and most importantly, they were paid for every patient they provided care for.

A new mother can be overwhelmed by all of the new responsibility she has in taking care of a new baby which makes a good pediatrician a very valuable resource for her. If she chooses one wisely, she will feel great relief that her child is getting superior care.

As children grow, they may face health challenges. Some could be life threatening and some could result in death. We as mothers may not be aware that our children face danger but we rely on the healthcare system to act quickly if emergency situations should arise.

Accidental Poisoning

We are always warned about the dangers of household cleaners and other things that we may keep in our home that must be kept away from children. There are warnings on the packaging of these items and the caps are made so that they are difficult for children to open. There are gadgets made to lock kitchen cabinets especially under the sink where these items are most commonly stored. Because of all of the precautions we practice today, we don't often hear about accidental poisonings. However, there are different things that a child or even an adult could ingest that could be very harmful. When this happens, it is critical that we have excellent medical personnel that can take swift action.

I know all too well how important this is as my twins were suspected of accidental poisoning when they were just fifteen months old. My husband was home sick and so that he could rest quietly, I took the children outside to play in our backyard. My son then two and a half years old, told me that the twins were eating something in the yard. They looked as if they were spitting out mushrooms that were growing next to our air conditioning unit. They were easy to miss as they were the same color as the unit blending into it.

I called poison control who recommended that I give them Ipecac Syrup and take the mushrooms to be identified by an expert since there are so many species. The expert owned a restaurant locally that specialized in mushroom delicacies and was a national recognized expert. He came out and briefly looked at the mushrooms and told me that he would have to do a little research and would call me.

As soon as I got home, the hospital emergency room called and told me to come right in with my twins. When we arrived, they immediately took us into a room with two doctors and three nurses. I was still telling myself that this was not a problem and everything would be ok. My pediatrician was on vacation and a middle-aged woman doctor always filled in for him. She suddenly walked into the emergency room and I heard her say "I just left a room full of patients in my waiting room, Joe knows his mushrooms and I think if that's what he says than we have to take this very seriously."

She got on the phone and it appeared that she was ordering an ambulance. I got up and walked to the back where the nurses and doctors were with my twins behind a curtain. I opened the curtain to see the doctor facing me and when I asked him what was wrong, he told me that it was fatal. I walked back to the area where the pediatrician was just getting off the phone. Calmly she quietly told me that she had just ordered an ambulance to take us down to St. Christopher's Children's Hospital in Philadelphia. I told her I didn't want them to be treated there that I would prefer if they can be treated in Reading. She said "we don't have the equipment here to handle this kind of emergency." She said it in such a way that she had me believing that they were just being overly cautious.

We spent two days down at St. Christopher's Hospital as they observed our twins and ran tests. We slept lightly through the night in a room with our twins and our son, sharing a room with terminally ill children that were never going home. The doctors determined that neither one of the twins had ingested the mushrooms and showed no effects of being poisoned and they were released. The species are known to taste bitter which is why they both spit them out.

I knew that the mushrooms that I had brought into the mushroom expert were poisonous but really didn't know how deadly they were. Five years later, one of my twins had an ear infection and my pediatrician was on vacation. The answering service suggested that I call the pediatrician that had dealt with our mushroom emergency.

"I don't know if you remember us but this is one of the twins who we suspected ate the poisonous mushrooms." I said.

"I will never forget you, that day was the worst day of my medical career. I went home and cried myself to sleep. I just could not stand the thought that I was going to have to tell you that not only one of your children would die but both would die."

I looked surprised and she said, "didn't you know, that species was so deadly that there was nothing we could do but put the twins on life support, that is why we transported them to St. Chris's."

When I first moved to Reading, there was an article in the Reading Eagle about a family of five sitting down to dinner to eat a mushroom delicacy. They considered themselves to be knowledgeable enough about mushrooms to go into wooded areas and pick the ones that are harmless and bring them home to cook. With spices, the bitter taste disappears. They had all died after eating the same species that I had growing in my backyard.

The year this emergency happened was 1985. We got the best care that we could have possibly gotten and everyone involved in this emergency gave it their best. The next story about an emergency room visit happened in 2002. It was during a time where we experienced a large influx of people from out of the area who routinely used emergency rooms as their primary care provider. By being uninsured they were able to take advantage of the Emergency Medical Treatment and Labor Act enacted in 1986. This is a federal law requiring anyone going to an emergency room be able to receive treatment regardless of whether or not they have insurance or the ability to pay. This encourages many to remain uninsured and use emergency rooms as their main health care provider resulting in a huge strain on our healthcare system.

Healthcare Today

As I got ready to leave a business luncheon, I experienced very sudden sharp chest pain. The pain became intense enough that I was afraid that I would pass out. I wondered if I should go to an emergency room or wait and hope it would go away. I also entertained the idea of going home which was fifteen miles away and secluded further away from any medical treatment in case I needed it. I left the restaurant and the pain continued. Somehow through the sharp chest pain I was experiencing, I got to the emergency room to find it filled with about fifty people. As I checked in, I told the woman at the check in that I had an emergency, very sharp chest pain.

"Take a number and you will be called when your number comes up," she said.

"Approximately what is the wait time" I asked.

"About three to four hours," she said.

"This is an emergency, I'm having very sharp chest pain, I feel like I might be having a heart attack."

"Yes, I understand that" she said, "you and all of the other people sitting here."

The room started to spin and I quickly sat down on the floor feeling as though I would pass out. There were no chairs left in the waiting room as they were all occupied.

"you can't sit on the floor, you will have to stand until a seat becomes available," she said

"I'm sorry, I can't do that, I'm afraid I'm going to pass out." I said.

There were twenty people waiting for seats and there wasn't likely to be one available for a long time. I listened to people checking in who came in and learned that not one of them had insurance. My husband left work and came in and waited with me. He had much of the same conversation with the receptionist that I had. We would just have to wait approximately three to four hours to be seen.

Sitting near the desk where people were checking in, from the conversations it became apparent that these people were using the emergency room as their primary care provider. When the receptionist asked who their insurance carrier was, they told her that they did not have insurance and they could not pay out of pocket. People were there for mostly coughs and colds looking for free samples so that they wouldn't have to purchase anything at a pharmacy. While we sat there, a doctor looking harried and worn out briskly walked out with a woman. She was screaming at the doctor calling him every name in the book when he turned to her and said, "no, I am not giving you pills, don't come in here again, you are a drug addict and you need a treatment center, not an emergency room,"

During the three to four hours I waited to be seen, I didn't see one case that looked like a true emergency. Finally, they called me back and I sat there and continued to wait. They saw the patient next to me who was there for a common cold and was asking for free samples of cold medicine. The person on the other side of me had indigestion and was also looking for free samples of medications. This definitely was no longer an emergency room but appeared to be a doctor's office for people with no insurance.

After an hour or more of waiting in a curtained area, someone came in to draw blood. I asked her when I would know the results. She said it would be approximately two and a half hours. I had come in early afternoon and now it was dark outside. I was starting to wonder if I would get home at any decent hour to get some sleep. She explained that they are very busy and because of the number of patients they have, it will take that long. I asked her if this is an unusually busy day and she told me it was like this every day. I settled back while the patients on either side of me left and were replaced with a few more patients. One had a sore throat and was looking for free throat lozenges and the other had a cough and was looking for free cough syrup.

The pain in my chest had subsided hours ago and I wondered what would have happened if it had not. The hospital that I had gotten such outstanding care from in the past was no longer capable of doing that. A doctor came in with an alarmed look on her face and told me that the blood test results had come back. She told me that my iron levels were alarmingly low and I was in danger of having a heart attack. She sent the results of the test to my primary physician recommending that I see him immediately, and prescribed iron tablets.

What happened to this emergency room as well as every other across the nation? The majority of people who were visiting them were not patients with emergencies but patients looking for free health care for common ailments. In the Reading area, they were mainly here illegally from Mexico or from New York. Many were unemployed with no health care insurance. The hospital staff had become desensitized to true emergencies and are treating all patients as though they have common ailments. Waiting to see a doctor three or four hours is unacceptable for any emergency room. Furthermore, the hospital emergency room was very understaffed for the number of patients walking in every day. Worse yet, the hospital is providing free health care to people who are not citizens while our citizens who have an emergency and contribute towards their group health care plan get the same substandard care. Hospitals could not go on like this. They still have to pay the employees who show up for work every day to take care of these patients who are receiving healthcare without paying a dime.

When patients carry no healthcare insurance the medical profession works pro bono. A few cases would not hurt our system but we are not talking about a few cases but instead, numbers that are staggering. As the medical field grew and equipment became state of the art, costs escalated to pay for this. At the same time, we have vast numbers of the population suffering from unemployment leaving them uninsured and pushing them down into income brackets which qualify them for Medicaid paying a lower rate for services than what is standard.

Hospitals cannot continue to provide free services so they have no alternative but to raise prices of services on the people who do pay to compensate for those who don't pay. The insurance carriers then must raise premiums to compensate for those raised prices in hospital services. The employers who provide healthcare coverage for their employees now must ask their employees to contribute towards the group plan that the employer contributes to due to rising premiums. Everyone gets the same level of care no matter what they are paying but eventually the level of care for everyone becomes substandard while premiums skyrocket for those who can pay. This is what we saw with healthcare reform under Obamacare.

Healthcare Reform

When healthcare reform was first introduced through Obamacare most people and especially those in the healthcare industry as well as the insurance industry knew that it wasn't the answer and certainly not the answer long term. The premiums on the healthcare exchange at first, were very cheap, in fact too cheap. It reminded me of the introductory offers we saw on mortgages for people who don't really qualify. The rate starts out very low but steadily increases until it is where it should be which is unaffordable. It steadily increases to the correct rate based on risk. However, healthcare reform was a little different in the sense that it was not based on risk but on income. Insurance whether we are talking about auto, life, health or most anything that would be insured has always been based on the risk that the insurance company is assuming.

While doing property management in low income neighborhoods it was very common to see young people do things that caused rapid health deterioration. They drank alcohol, did "recreational drugs", ate poorly and led a sedentary life with no exercise. They made bad life decisions which caused stress leading to being overweight. That in turn led to high cholesterol, high blood pressure, diabetes, sleep disorders, and numerous other health issues. This leads to dysfunction of major organs in their bodies requiring constant medical care. It was common to see women wearing adult diapers by the time they were in their early fifties paid for through Medicaid and mailed to them monthly. People who fall into this health category would be considered by any health insurance carrier to be in a "high risk" category. Those high-risk people who are also low income cannot afford the premium to be insured. Obamacare was designed to get them healthcare insurance, paid for by the middle class.

Small business owners earning between $70,000 and $120,000 were hurt by Obamacare very badly. Many of these small business owners started a business after being laid off from a job with an employer covering them under a group plan. This leaves them buying healthcare insurance on the insurance exchange. For those in that income category their premiums for a family could be as high as $20,000 per year. If they are earning $70,000 for instance, they are knocked down to an annual income of $50,000. For someone earning between $70,000 and $120,000, this is a lot of money to pay for healthcare insurance, especially if they are in good health and don't use it. As premiums escalated, insureds in this income category were forced to make a decision between paying their monthly mortgage payment or paying for healthcare insurance. This forced many to drop their healthcare insurance resulting in skyrocketing premiums for those that remained in the plan in that income category. If they are fortunate enough to find an employer offering group healthcare insurance, they are leaving a small business that they love and are meant to do to work at a job they dislike just for healthcare insurance. I saw many in the trades go out of business and work for a home center because they were getting healthcare benefits through that employer. If they were to stay in business it meant working longer hours to pay for healthcare insurance. Many young people have been advised by their parents not to go into the trades because of the expense of healthcare insurance. That leaves a shortage of workers such as plumbers, electricians and carpenters who generally fall into that income category.

While at a party one evening I was talking with a single man in his fifties when Obamacare was first introduced. He had been self-employed most of his life and chose not to carry healthcare insurance because he never used it. He was in excellent health and never got sick. When he visited his doctor for annual physicals, he paid out of pocket which was a lot less than paying monthly insurance premiums. He was very angry that he was forced into buying healthcare insurance and instead chose to pay the fine. I asked him what the premium would be if he were to buy insurance on the exchange. For a high deductible plan, before premiums escalated, he would be paying $125 per month. I pointed out that $125 was very cheap in comparison to what he would have paid before healthcare reform. He said he really didn't care about that because he had never paid for healthcare insurance. The fine would be $1500 per year. Would paying $125 a month and being insured not be better than paying $1500 per year and not being insured at all? He explained that the premium would never stay at $125 per month. I suggested that he at least pay the $125 per month and be insured until the premiums escalate and then drop it. At least he would have coverage for a time. He pointed out that most likely, he would never reach the deductible so he would still be paying everything out of pocket like he always had and in addition, $125 per month which would not be benefitting him at all.

Healthcare reform needed many people like this man for it to work especially if they were to insure people who were uninsurable. Many like this man chose to pay the fine instead of contributing to the plan from the very beginning. Some chose to be insured but as the premiums escalated, they dropped out. The policy holders remaining in the plan were very high risk paying the lowest premiums. Insurance carriers dropped out of the Marketplace leaving very few plans to choose from which caused premiums to skyrocket since there was no competition to keep them low. This single man's premium that was once $125 a month has escalated to $900 per month presently.

Obamacare has placed an enormous burden on both the medical field and the insurance industry. It has forced both to implement a set of metrics to measure productivity of their employees and to adopt work requirements that are possible by only a few. As a result, many that were at one time considered to be good employees, now fell below the expectation and were terminated. Hospitals and insurance companies lose money every day on people who do not contribute their fair share resulting in the employees having to work harder with much less.

Medicaid

Medicaid is health insurance for low income people either single or families provided for by our government through the taxes that we pay. The costs that are the most draining under Medicaid are drug treatment and elderly care. The average drug treatment center during 2009-2016 when drugs poured into the country at an alarming rate was $30,000, a month per person. Considering the large number of people who were in need of drug treatment, this is an astronomical cost that we all contribute to. Now add to this cost the number of non-citizens who also use treatment centers. When considering that a stay in a treatment center could be up to two years at a cost of $30,000 per month, the cost for one person is on average $720,000. Many relapse and keep going back to treatment to repeat that cost over and over for just one person. When we consider the number of people who struggle with drug addiction, the amount paid for by our government is staggering.

Many of these people land in nursing homes under Medicaid which is safer for them than living on the street where most never really recover from their addictions. The vast number of undocumented people who come to our country to collect welfare, food stamps and get free health care will eventually transition into a nursing home under Medicaid where our system will be further and greatly drained as skilled nursing homes are the most expensive health care people receive in their lifetime depending on the number of years they live.

Stella

I met Stella through real estate when she called me to do a broker's price opinion on her mother's home that was being sold since her mother was going to a nursing home. After her father died ten years previously, she had transferred ownership of the home to herself and her brother to avoid inheritance tax at her mother's death. Stella divided up the small savings that her mother had for the same reason since her mother's social security was more than adequate for her living expenses. Stella and her brother were at a stage in their lives where that extra money was not needed but did come in handy to put in a new kitchen in her house as well as some other luxuries. With that money being spent instead of invested, and the home being transferred out of her mother's name, her mother was considered to be financially destitute and qualified for Medicaid. Stella was proud of herself and was thinking about writing a book that would advise people on how to successfully transfer nursing home care cost to the government. This is when nursing home costs covered under Medicaid becomes expensive because this person has a longer life expectancy than the person who truly does qualify for Medicaid.

Medicare for All

Medicare is healthcare insurance for our senior citizens who are over sixty-five years of age. They have contributed to Medicare for years during the time that they worked. Medicare Part A covers hospital costs and Part B or Medicare Advantage covers doctor's visits. Part B or Medicare Advantage is paid for by the insured, their premium depending on what they contributed through the years and deducted from their monthly social security check. I'm confused when people say they want Medicare for All because we already have a form of that under Obamacare which is failing. I think what they really mean is "Medicaid for All" which would be free healthcare for everyone.

Under proposed free healthcare plans many seniors would no longer be covered under Medicare but instead, their healthcare would be replaced with a universal Medicaid plan with the costs being rolled into increased taxes for every tax bracket. This is especially a burden on our seniors who are living on a fixed income as well as the middle class. For those people who are working and covered under a group plan through private insurance, that plan would also go away.

Many doctors refuse to take Medicare and Medicaid because of the low reimbursement rate, the administrative burdens and claim processing delays. The ones who do limit their practice to a few of these patients and charge patients with private insurance more for services to compensate for these disadvantages. With private insurance going away under a proposed free healthcare plan a career in medicine will become less desirable leaving shortages of medical providers and healthcare much like what I have described in my visit to an emergency room in 2002. Free sounds great but if there are no providers, it becomes a plan that no one can afford.

Socialized Medicine

While vacationing in Europe where socialized medicine exists, my ninety-year old father in law fell off a tour bus on his shoulder. A relative who practices medicine in the United States who was with him told him he needed X rays and an MRI. After waiting to see a doctor for three hours, they told him that they can't see him for three days since it is not an emergency. When three days goes by and he does have the procedures that he needs, they tell him that he will have to wait a week for someone to read his results. By that time, he would be back in the United States. His daughter made an appointment for him for the day after he came home from vacation where the procedure and the results were completed in one day. That is the difference in the healthcare we have today in the United States and the healthcare that Europe has that is being proposed for us here in America. For us to insure people who are uninsurable as well as people who are here illegally and don't pay a dime for healthcare means that we have to pay more through increased taxes. We also have to be willing to accept substandard healthcare. If my twins had been poisoned, they would have had a slimmer chance of survival under the proposed healthcare.

Planned Parenthood

Planned Parenthood clinics are found in urban areas with the purpose of providing family planning counseling, birth control, pregnancy resources, abortion, and STD treatment to low income women residents. They are within walking distance to provide easy accessibility. The amount that patients pay for services depends on their income. To determine the value of any service like Planned Parenthood, we have to look at what procedures they routinely perform and for who.

In Reading, Planned Parenthood was located on the corner of So. 4th St. and Franklin St. a one-way street traveling east and running parallel to the main street,

Penn St. To avoid the traffic on Penn St, I used Franklin St. every day to do maintenance checks on properties I managed on the south side of Reading. From observation, Planned Parenthood seemed to have no activity except on Tuesdays when a doctor came up from Philadelphia to perform abortions while protestors stood out front holding pictures of aborted babies.

Over the years, I noticed that there are a lot of myths surrounding Planned Parenthood. Many will argue that it is a valuable service to victims of rape, victims of incest, or girls too young to have a baby. I have known many women who have had abortions and not one fitting the profile of being pregnant as the result of a rape or incest. I'm sure they exist but they are exceptions to the rule. I have known many young girls that I believe are too young to have a baby but I have never seen one consider having an abortion. The babies that they had were delivered at one of our hospitals with services being paid by Medicaid. I have seen couples have a child that they could not afford and gave the baby up for adoption at birth.

The women that I saw most commonly use Planned Parenthood were to either treat an STD or to perform an abortion. They were working the streets to support a drug habit and were at the highest risk for pregnancy. The second group of women who were likely to use Planned Parenthood for abortion services were single women over the age of forty paying minors for sex and got pregnant. Their own children were older than the minor who got them pregnant and they needed to get rid of the pregnancy immediately before anyone found out. They would tell me that they were going to be late paying rent because they needed to get an abortion and needed to pay something towards the cost. Both of these groups were repeat customers having abortions due to illegal activity and that is what has to be considered when decisions are made about whether or not the government should fund Planned Parenthood versus the cases that are the exceptions.

15

THE GIFT OF LIFE

Through the human race flows a mighty stream of
potential life.
Out of this, God called me to be a person, different
from all others.
What a wonder! What a mystery is this! That I should
be myself?
Was it chance that called me to live?
Or was it the election of God's love and grace that
called me into being?
And surrounded me with human love?
Gratitude wells up within my heart for this great gift of
life.
Like changing season, a human life is gone too soon.
A tiny segment of time, but I have lived and I have
loved and life is not contained by time alone
It is woven into the fabric of eternity.

By Gladys B. Metzger

My paternal grandmother was the author of this as it
was found in her handwriting and signed by her,
amongst her belongings after she died. I am in awe
when I read this and realize that very few receive the
gift of life. The chances of making it to conception are
very slim and then the question is that if we make it

that far, will our life be allowed to continue. I almost missed out on the gift of life twice but the decisions that both of my great grandmothers made, eventually resulted in my life.

The author, my grandmother, married a man who was born out of wedlock in 1888. His mother gave birth to him when she was just nineteen years old, never marrying the father. The father was nine years older, never married and had a life of many business accomplishments. Abortion was available and done routinely until it was illegal in around 1900 being an option for her that she didn't choose. She had her baby, raising him by herself until she later married someone else and had seven more children.

My maternal great grandmother on the other side of my family was married and had many children. There were some miscarriages and then there was my grandmother, another miscarriage that produced a live birth. The doctor said that it was the smallest live baby that he had ever delivered. He advised her not to get too attached as she had no real chance of survival. My great grandmother fought for her child's life doing everything possible to help her survive. My grandmother grew up, married a wonderful man and had my mother and her sister living into her nineties.

My grandparents stopped by to check on her parents at dinner time one evening and found them splitting a can of peaches. When she asked if that was all they were having for dinner, they said that it was all they could afford as the rent was due in a few days. My grandmother told her parents that they would give up their rented home and move in with her and live with her for the rest of their lives, never having to worry about not getting enough to eat again as they had lived in poverty most of their lives. My grandparents were raising their own children at home but never looked at her parents as being a burden. There were many other children who helped by giving money towards their parent's care, but my grandmother insisted that her parents would live with her. My grandmother fought for her parents lives as they had once fought for her tiny life. These are the values that we pass down from one generation to the next. When we stop having moral values regarding life, it erodes our society as a whole. If my grandmother's life was not valued by her parents, she would not have valued their lives as elderly people causing her to make different choices regarding their care.

16

SOCIAL PROGRAMS

With more and more people remaining unemployed after the housing crisis with no end in sight, this caused more people than ever to become dependent on a variety of government programs.

Supplemental Nutrition Assistance Program (food stamps)

This program provides nutritional benefits to supplement the food budget of needy families so they can purchase healthy food and move towards self-sufficiency. Since the downturn of the economy, food stamp collection was extended to many single unemployed people as well. One of the questions on my application for an apartment asked if applicants were collecting food stamps and the amount they were collecting. This question was asked to determine their overall income to get an idea as to whether or not they could afford the apartment.

I had observed enormous amounts of food being wasted and thrown out in comparison to how I had grown up. My parent's finances were very lean when I was a child but we had enough. To stay within a set amount allocated for food for our family my mother cooked everything from scratch and purchased no prepackaged expensive items. We never threw any food out and if we didn't finish our meal, our parents finished it for us.

As a child, I noticed as we stood in line at the grocery store to pay for our groceries, many carts filled to the brim with all the treats that I so much craved that my mother told me we could not afford. All of these people paid with money that looked like play money instead of the regular cash my mother used to pay for our groceries with. When I asked why they were paying with different money she explained that they were paying with food stamps which was what people received from the government because they were poor. Then I would watch them load those numerous bags of groceries into a new Cadillac like my neighbor had who was involved in illegal activity.

One night after one of those grocery trips with my mother I asked my father if we could get food stamps. The way I saw it as a very young child was that with our few groceries and old car, we were definitely poorer than those people driving away in a luxury car with lots of groceries including fresh lobster, filet mignon, soda and lots of prepackaged cakes and cookies. My father said, "If you are dependent as an adult on anyone, you will never be great."

I would see many of my tenants who collected food stamps standing in a soup kitchen line about a week and a half before they received their next benefit. While they stood in line, they talked on a cell phone. In addition to food stamps and soup kitchens, many would collect food donations at food pantries. When they moved out of my apartment it was common to see both the refrigerator and kitchen cabinets filled with food left behind.

Trash Collection

I opened my trash bill for the month which showed a $90 overage fee on the building that is in the poorest neighborhood in the city. I found that the poorer the neighborhood, the higher the trash bill. It was clearly written in the lease that they were not to throw out household items but only trash which would be mostly disposable food items. This was always a problem since many of their belongings had a very short life. Household items that I had purchased had a lifetime life for me but only on average, three months life for my tenants.

I called my trash company and asked what specifically the overage was. They told me that the trash cans were over the allowable weight which was the reason for the overcharge. After getting a few monthly bills with this overage charge, I did a maintenance check on that building one hour before trash was picked up on trash day.

I dumped trash cans and canned goods in perfect condition rolled out of the trash can. I counted a total of 150 cans. I donated many to the Salvation Army and then would think I was finding the same cans in my trash again. Just for curiosity sake, I marked the cans and sure enough, they kept turning up in the trash as this went on week after week.

I had asked every tenant if they were dumping canned goods in the trash and of course everyone denied it. I couldn't figure out why anyone would take donations and throw them in the trash until a tenant explained it to me. Those cans came from a food bank as well as the Salvation Army. They were part of a package which included mostly canned goods and some boxes of cereal. No one wanted the canned goods but they kept going to the food bank for the cereal. They would take the cereal and throw the rest out.

Another problem I found with the trash was most of last evening's dinner being thrown out. Large pots of food were cooked on the stove without any thought of how many people would be eating. After it sat on the stove for a few days instead of being wrapped up and refrigerated immediately after dinner, it would be put in a large garbage bag and tossed out the window, missing the can while the bag broke spilling the contents all over the ground. Since the building was my responsibility and no one would own up to it, I would have to clean it up constantly or get fined by the city.

On a maintenance check I found a beautiful cake out on the back porch. It had been someone's birthday and two thirds of the cake was left over. Not having adequate storage, it was moved to the back porch. I recognized it from an expensive neighborhood bakery. The cake I estimated cost about $60. It had rained the night before on the cake ruining it leaving the tenant no alternative but to throw the leftover cake out. Just in that instance, they had thrown out $40. A better choice would have been to cut the cake in serving portions and store in plastic containers in the freezer. For someone relying on government assistance, buying a cake at a gourmet bakery is what keeps people poor. A better choice would have been to buy a box mix and icing and make the cake yourself. Instead of $60 it would have cost $3 or less if bought on sale or a store brand purchased.

Another reason that many ran out of food stamp money before the next allocation was that they sold their food stamps on the street for a fraction of their value so that they could buy drugs, alcohol and cigarettes and then relied on food banks and charities to feed them for the rest of the month. The more they received, the more they threw out. I don't think that there is any question that many people do qualify for food stamps due to low income however, we also must be aware of the fraud that goes on in the food stamp program as well as many other programs.

Fraud

Around the end of my mother's teaching career in early 1990's she worked with another teacher who was collecting food stamps. My mother found out when she stopped into the grocery store to pick up a few groceries on her way home from work. This teacher was also doing the same thing and paying with food stamps. My mother happened to be behind her in line and was so embarrassed for her that she hid behind the magazine rack before she was noticed. This teacher lived in an upscale neighborhood and owned a more expensive home than my parents did. So how would she ever be eligible for food stamps? I could not help but think of the young people I sold homes to who worked so hard to save for a down payment for a home while paying taxes to fund food stamps for someone owning a home that was valued at a much higher cost than the home they were attempting to save for. I have heard many stories like this over the years and have heard many scenarios on how people have somehow beat the system to make this happen.

Fraud runs openly rampant in the free school lunch program. I have known many teachers as well as cafeteria workers who have voiced their disapproval of the way the free or reduced lunch program works. It is difficult to understand how a family can own a $350,000 home in an area where the average price of a home is $250,000 and the children in that household are receiving free or reduced lunch. Some have told me that there are no requirements other than signing your child up.

Housing Vouchers

I have signed a number of housing vouchers for tenants over the years. Some fall under the Section 8 program but others fall under other city and county programs. I had a tenant who received a housing voucher for two years through a program where more than half of her rent was paid. She worked full time and should not have needed this voucher at all with careful budgeting. She struggled from the beginning paying her small portion of the rent. Within four months of moving into the apartment, I had to file for eviction for nonpayment of her portion. She immediately called the codes department with a list of problems that did not exist in the apartment. She got caught up and then behind again and I went through the eviction process all over. She became belligerent in court and then filed an appeal. She dragged the appeal out until the housing voucher was over costing me legal fees to hire an attorney to move the eviction forward. If she got evicted her housing voucher would end before collecting the entire two years.

Instead of focusing on getting something for free, why not focus on bettering yourself to get a better job or budget your money so you don't have to play games. Her portion of the rent was so cheap that it would be impossible to find an apartment for what she was paying. The housing voucher she received made her a nasty person. She looked at me as a threat the entire time she had the voucher and as soon as it ended, she went back to being decent since there was nothing to fight with me about. Yes, I understood how a person will never be great if they are dependent.

Contents Allowance

I became aware of a program between 2009 and 2015 for a housing contents allowance for low income people moving to a new apartment. The allowance was good for one year and they would be eligible again in another year to collect that contents allowance again. To receive that allowance, you would have to show proof of moving through your new lease and a form signed by your landlord. During that time, I had the highest turnover I had ever experienced as this allowance encouraged people to move every year leaving a whole apartment of contents behind since they were receiving all new contents. It was broken and dirty which meant it would not be able to be sold in a consignment shop, yard sale, or online. It would not be able to be donated because of the condition it was in after just one year.

During the Obama election there were booths set up around the city for free cell phones. The phones were offered for a limited time period and at the end of that time period they would have to start paying for them. I found that when the free period ended and my tenants had to start paying for them and refused to give them up, I had more evictions than I have ever had. Giving someone something they can't afford that they will eventually have to pay for is not improving the lives of those people.

Heating Allowance

With the influx of people from out of the area and many from Mexico as well as other warmer areas, I found that they were unable to adjust to our cold winters. They wore summer clothing with no sweater or sweatshirt and expected me to turn the heat up to a temperature that they were accustomed to such as ninety degrees. This heat was a constant battle until I had electric baseboard heating installed and passed the expense onto the tenant. After they controlled the heat I would drive by and see windows wide open when temperatures outside were below freezing. When I entered those particular apartments, the heat was cranked up as high as it could go. The large amount of usage incurred resulted in unpaid bills for the utility companies. Instead of putting on warmer clothing heating assistance was applied for and granted.

Clothing Waste

When tenants moved out of my apartments it was common for me to dispose of contractor bags filled with clothing somewhere between 20-50, 30 gal bags. This was a typical amount for a family of four consisting of two adults and two children. This occurs through impulse buying with no plan in place of what exactly would be needed. I observed numerous trendy outfits that would be worn once or twice before being thrown out leaving no money for necessary items such as underwear, socks, and basic items that would last until they were worn out.

An Easter Dress

I was doing a last maintenance check for an apartment that had just been completely cleaned out, painted and repaired. I opened a closet and there hanging was a beautiful Easter dress. I stood and stared at the dress as I recalled a memory from my childhood. I was around six years old when my mother and I went to a department store to shop for an Easter dress. My mother immediately headed to the clearance racks while I wondered around the newly arrived Easter dresses so eloquently displayed. I looked up at the most beautiful Easter dress that I had ever seen.

My mother stood behind me and asked, "Where will you ever wear that besides for Easter?"

"To church," I replied

"There are only a few Sundays until summertime and if we miss church those few Sundays, you won't get enough wear out of it." she said.

"I can wear it when we are on vacation in the summer and go out for dinner." I suggested

"It will be too hot with those short little sleeves in it for summertime." she responded.

"Then I can wear it after the summer," I said

"It is a very springy dress and would not look right in the fall," she said

"Well then I can wear it next spring," I said

"By then you will have outgrown it" she replied

My mother always chose a sleeveless dress of Navy blue and a white sweater which could be worn spring, summer and fall. As I continued to stare at the beautiful Easter dress in the closet, I thought of the tenant that had resided there. It was a husband, wife and two daughters ages four and one. They both worked and both children attended the daycare on site where she worked. The husband failed a drug test at work and was fired from his job. She threw him out of the apartment but could not financially manage on her own. I noticed during a maintenance check that all the garbage and trash was thrown in a corner loosely and not bagged in a trash bag let alone a kitchen trash receptacle. She told me that she couldn't afford trash bags or a trash container. The baby sat most of the day in a heavily soiled diaper because she was always running out of diapers. When the daycare bill didn't get paid, she took her husband back who watched the kids during the day while she went to work. After he came back the trash bags and diapers still remained a problem. The five-year old started kindergarten and the husband would walk her to school every morning while he pushed the baby in a stroller. After dropping the older child at school, he would come home, put the baby in her crib for the rest of the day with a bottle, and get high with four of his friends. That went on most of the day until it was time to pick the older one up from school. The apartment was filthy and the children slept in filth. The sheets were never washed on their beds, and the children wore heavily soiled clothes.

During the Christmas season, they fell behind in rent so that they could buy toys for the kids. The kids had so many toys in the apartment that you could barely walk through, not to mention the many trash bags filled with clothes. The wife became angry when she incurred late fees and told me I should give them a break because it is just her working and they are struggling. The late fee for being six days late was $30 and that fee doubled to $60 after being 11 days late. That following spring they left the apartment when they fell too far behind leaving all of the contents behind.

As I stared at the beautiful Easter dress hanging before me, I reached over for the tag that was still on the dress indicating that it had never been worn. It was a size twelve months, obviously a dress for the baby that she would never wear. The price tag read $60 which was the exact amount of the late fee. In other words, I should cut them a break on the late fee so that they can use that money to buy items they can't afford to throw them in the trash.

In the past, many tenants after being evicted, would move in with a relative to save for another first month's rent and security deposit. They would move all of the contents in their apartment within thirty days because by law I could dispose of it after that. With the new programs in place, as long as they had stayed in my apartment for a year, they were eligible for a first month's rent and security deposit as well as contents allowance fully funded by our government. This encouraged tenants to move every year causing landlords high turnover as well as increased expenses for disposal.

17

THE COST OF INHERITANCE TAX

As states look for ways to fund social programs, the first place they look at are people who have extra money they can take through taxes. A good source is the elderly who have accumulated wealth that they tax in the form of an inheritance tax when they die. The reason why this segment of the population has accumulated wealth is usually not because they had high paying jobs or inherited it themselves but is the result of the life decisions they made as well as being very good at managing their money.

Inheritance tax opens up a lot of business for estate attorneys, financial planners, and tax accountants. Like any other profession some are good and some are not. The best worked a long time to establish a business with a clientele that they regularly serve. Many have recently entered the profession and are looking to build their business which means that they are salespeople more than anything else.

Professionals selling financial advice

Many professionals find their clientele through other professionals for a referral fee. They are not referred for reasons of expertise but reasons of which professional is the highest bidder. For those people who don't do their own research as well as make their own choices, they most always come up with a professional who costs them more money in the long run. The best referrals come from close friends or relatives who have used that service and are not benefitting monetarily for making the recommendation. The best professionals are excellent at what they do and don't need to pay for new clients.

Some professionals offer a one stop shopping service where they try to do it all. They get a law license, a real estate license, a securities license, etc. Instead of focusing on what they do best and finding clients that they can serve, they try to be all of the things to fewer clients. Clients never receive the best service when they rely on this type of one stop shopping.

Financial Planning and Free Dinners

A popular way for new professionals to obtain business is to offer a free dinner in exchange to listening to estate planning advice. They send out a mass mailing to selective zip codes with buzz phrases such as "avoid tax at your death," "preserve your estate," "shelter your estate," or something of that nature. They are looking for people who have accumulated enough money in retirement plans or other savings plans that make it worth their time to pursue. There are few new clients they meet at these dinners, but when they get one it more than pays for all of the dinners. Not only are they new clients for financial planners but they can refer them for a fee to estate attorneys or accountants. Many people are led to believe that they need to take urgent action to avoid costs associated with death which is what encourages them to set up meetings with professional people in the first place. The tax law is complex and changes constantly so relying on information from other people no matter who they are may not be correct and can be very costly. There are free publications that can be requested from the IRS which will be most accurate. Before meeting with anyone I would have an idea of the tax law and a general idea of its effect on your personal situation since everyone's is different.

Lack of knowledge and Bad Timing

I had done a lot of business with a family over about twenty years so I was able to see how their decisions early on affected their estate, leaving their mother financially destitute at the end of her life. Her husband held a position with a large company and also invested in real estate rental units generating income. He had contributed a good portion of his income to savings and retirement plans. At age sixty-eight, three years after the husband retired, he had a sudden heart attack and died leaving behind two adult sons as well as a wife. The sons and the mother were faced with wealth that none of them had any knowledge on how to manage so they enlisted the help of a financial advisor for advice.

The financial advisor talked with them about inheritance tax and recommended that they see an estate attorney that he works closely with to guide them in avoiding it. The attorney recommended taking steps to shelter the mother's money by first selling her primary residence as well as all other real estate she owned. Then taking the proceeds in addition to all of her investments and placing them in trust and then gifting that money every year to her sons to alleviate inheritance tax for them upon her death. By doing this she would be able to live at the best assisted living facility in the area where many of her friends were living covered by Medicaid since she would be considered financially destitute by the state. The mother assumed that her room in the assisted living facility would be a luxurious apartment similar to the rooms of her friends residing there who were self-pay residents. Instead it was very small in a basement wing of the facility with no windows.

I have seen a growing increase of people turning to estate planners with similar solutions to what I have described above since the downturn of the economy. Many attorneys and estate planners have entered the job market pushing a need for estate planning to avoid expenses associated with death. This has created employment for them at the expense of the tax payers. A better solution would have been for the mother to keep all of her money and invest it wisely so that she could go into assisted living on her terms if that is what she wanted to do. She could have the most beautiful 2200 square foot apartment with lots of windows overlooking the most beautiful scenery imaginable, like my great aunt had instead of what she got. Furthermore, had that money not been touched, it would have grown substantially making the cost of that apartment miniscule in comparison to the wealth she would have accumulated in the twenty-five more years that she lived after her husband died.

When politicians constantly propose increasing inheritance tax to fund government programs, it encourages many to seek advice from financial planners. Aside from the fact that our parents already paid tax on that money and their children should not be taxed again, there is a much bigger and costlier problem than that. The government will pick up the tab for the parent's care that they could have well afforded and in a much more quality way, if that money was left alone until the parent's death. If there was no inheritance tax (which is how these discussions with estate planners start) there would be no reason for people to go looking for ways to reduce it where they would get into discussions with financial planners on transferring nursing home care costs to the government. Our government cannot afford to support the elderly that can afford to support themselves as those people usually live a lot longer than someone who has spent their life in poverty that truly does qualify for Medicaid. The cost then gets transferred to everyone through our increasing health care costs which is another reason why the cost of health care has skyrocketed.

In real estate transactions I was involved in I found that timing had a lot to do with whether or not an estate was preserved for future generations. The estate was most likely to be preserved if inherited no sooner than age sixty-five. There was a better chance if the beneficiaries were over age seventy. That put their children in their forties and most likely, financially independent and responsible

The next cases represent two families spanning four generations. Their stories defy what I just said about the timing of inheritances, because of course there are always exceptions to every rule. The first generations immigrated from Europe in the 1870's and purchased farms in Pennsylvania of the same size two miles apart from each other. At the time of the sale of these farms, one was worth $360,000 and the other sold for $1,500,000. The reason for the difference in price was that they were sold twenty-six years apart. The family that came out ahead had nothing to do with price and everything to do with the decisions that were made by the third generation at the time that they were sold.

A TALE OF TWO FARMS

Farm #1

The first generation immigrated from Ireland in the 1870's to escape starvation and poverty in their country. They had an opportunity in America for a better life where there was no war over religion and plenty to eat if they owned a farm. They were grief stricken over the death of three children due to the severe starvation in their country. They longed for children and that was another hope that they had for themselves living in America.

When they arrived in America, they worked very hard on their dairy farm. Several years later, they had a daughter whom they named Patricia. Life was very good for them in America. They lived the rest of their lives on their farm where they raised their daughter. Patricia grew up, got married and raised a boy and a girl. Patricia and her husband owned a home building business where they both worked hard and made a good living.

When Patricia and her husband were in their early sixties her husband died after a long illness. Her home was free and clear and they had savings invested that kept Patricia in a comfortable lifestyle. When Patricia was in her seventies, both her parents passed away leaving her the farm. It took Patricia several years to clean the farmhouse out to prepare it for sale. Her children were not nearly as ambitious as she was so she had no help from them. Meanwhile, Patricia was paying taxes and upkeep on the farm during the time that she was getting it ready for sale while her children bickered with each other over the contents in the farmhouse. The sale eventually brought $1,500,000 for the farm in 2006. Patricia's children were very excited about that money and expected to both get a portion of it. Patricia's son Patrick had grown up and married and had a life of his own with a family, but Patricia's daughter Reagan had spent her adult life living with her mother. Reagan's husband had not had steady employment for periods of time which left Reagan working and dependent on her mother for child care while her two children were growing up. When the farm was sold, Reagan talked her mother into buying a home in a neighborhood where the average price was $1,200,000. That tied up a good portion of the inheritance in addition to what they felt would appreciate in leaps and bounds. This made no sense considering that no one in that family had employment that could really support a home in that price range.

In 2009, when the market rapidly declined, they put the home on the market and tried to sell it for what they paid for it. When they were unable to sell it, they took a reverse mortgage which was the only thing they could do to get a hold of the equity. They did not have the option of giving the home back to the bank as they had tied up $1,200,000 in cash into it. This prevented them from investing that money any further in anything else. All real estate requires constant repair which is a problem if housing is not proportionate to the owner's income. Obviously, these people not having an income that fit this housing were using some of the inheritance money to make needed repairs as well as for living expenses depleting that money and making it unavailable for further investing. The value of the home was not increasing because of the economy and the repairs needed, mostly maintenance items such as a new roof and heating system. All of that is expected to be in working order or they have to be able to purchase the home at a price that reflects those repairs needed. No matter what cash they had put into this home, the home would still maintain the same value and would be unavailable for other investments.

Continuing in this financial plan will deplete this estate leaving nothing for future generations.

Farm #2

I first met Barry and Jill when they came to one of my Sunday open houses. The neighborhood in which they lived was a typical average neighborhood that sold well during that period of time. It was not known as the best school district but a fairly average one. Their home was a three bedroom two and a half bath, with a two-car garage. Nothing about it stood out that would be long remembered after the sale. What was so unusual about this couple is what they were buying. The home that I sold them was in a price range that most prudent people such as Jill and Barry would not feel comfortable buying. Jill and Barry were much the same way as the home they sold, very average people. They were in their mid-fifties with two children who were self-supporting and living on their own. Barry had an average job earning an average income and Jill did not work. As we stood in the home that I sold to them admiring the view out the master bedroom window, I couldn't help but notice how average these people really were. Jill's shoes and clothing were slightly dated but neat and clean and she looked well put together. They had arrived at the property in a four door Buick sedan.

The first generation to occupy this farm started out exactly like the first generation of the first farm. They immigrated from Ireland to escape starvation and poverty in their country. The first generation was a newly married couple hoping to raise children and live a long and prosperous life in America. Every couple of years they had a baby, each time a boy. They had four boys and longed for a girl. At last, the fifth child was a girl. When the baby girl was three months old, there was a fire in their farm house which killed all four of their sons sleeping in a bedroom above the kitchen where the fire originated. The parents were sleeping in a bedroom at the opposite end of the house with their baby in a cradle beside their bed. They were able to escape with their baby girl, but their four sons were trapped in the house and perished. The couple never had any more children.

The little girl grew up, got married and lived nearby with her husband. They raised a boy and a girl several years apart. When they were teenagers, the boy was diagnosed with leukemia and eventually died. The girl, Jill, grew up and went to a college an hour away. While attending college, she met her husband, Barry, and after college they found jobs, married, and settled there. Within several years, Jill and Barry bought a small modest home in a desirable neighborhood and started a family. Meanwhile, Jill's grandparents were getting up in years and Jill's parents, living nearby, were able to look after them. Eventually, both grandparents died and Jill's parents were busy cleaning out the old farm house that they had occupied to prepare it for sale.

The farm house included 75 acres of land which caught the attention of a nearby developer. Jill's parents and the developer were in negotiations on the farm, and the plan was to sell to that developer as soon as they cleaned the personal belongings of the grandparents out of the house. The year was 1983 and the value of the farm was around $350,000. The developer and Jill's parents were all in agreement to sell the farm for that amount of money. On the last trip they had made cleaning out the home, Jill's parents were both instantly killed in a head on collision by a drunk driver driving on the wrong side of the highway. Jill inherited the farm and the land at the age of thirty-three. Selling this farm to the developer could have put Jill into a very different lifestyle. She was so devastated over the death of her parents that she did nothing for several years. The builder had contacted Jill on a number of occasions to sell the farm and in the year 1986, the farm had increased in value due to a real estate boom. The builder was very much in agreement to compensating Jill well for that appreciation.

After Jill's grief somewhat subsided, she began to think of the possibility of subdividing this land herself and selling off lots privately since building lots were in such demand. Over the next twenty years, that is exactly what she did. Jill and Barry had moved to a larger home several years before her grandparents died, and continued to live in that home without using any of the money from the lot sales to buy a better home or lifestyle. Jill was very involved in raising her children and they excelled in school and later in life. During the years that Jill invested the money it grew substantially. Jill and Barry sent their daughters to top colleges not using any of the money they had inherited, but from their own savings. The home that I sold for them had been recently paid off, which was nothing extraordinary considering that they had lived there twenty-five years. They were using the proceeds from that and borrowing the rest of the money against an investment account. When I requested a verification of funds, the investment company sent me a copy of the statement of the account that they were borrowing from. It showed a balance of $12,000,000. I figured that it was a typographical error and didn't pay a lot of attention to it. When Jill found out that they had sent me the statement showing the full balance she called me and asked me to please never tell anyone about their wealth. They had wanted to just mainstream into society without drawing any attention to themselves which they had done quite well. She explained to me how that money gave her peace of mind for many years, knowing that her job of selling building lots gave her the flexibility to work and also the time to take care of her family.

For many, they would lack the vision to grow an estate that would turn out anything like what I have just described and especially at a very young age. If Jill and Barry had sold the farm and used all of that money to buy a better home for themselves as in the first example, the best that their net worth could be, would be $1,500,000 instead of $12,000.000, quite a big difference.

18

A CULTURE OF ANGER AND HATE

July 2015

The female voice on the other end of the phone was answering an ad for an available apartment. She pleasantly answered my questions I asked as part of my screening process. The apartment was for her and her mother, the mother's income was disability and the daughter worked at a nearby retail store. I agreed to meet them later in the afternoon and show them the apartment. I was surprised to find out that the female voice was actually male. Chris was meticulously and neatly dressed and had a very warm personality. I did not have the same good feeling about his mother. I rented the apartment to them and he was one of my best tenants. He would often call and ask if he could change things in the apartment at his expense. He was very particular and took great pride in the apartment. About a year later, his sister got in a jam and needed a place to live. I rented her the apartment across the hall because I liked him so much. Her source of income was disability so I figured there should not be a problem with the rent since her income came regularly on the third of the month. I had the same feeling about her as I had for the mother which was not good. In a short period of time, her apartment was crawling with roaches and the new rented furniture was filthy. She had three children and a boyfriend whom eventually got her evicted when he stole her rent money. In the year that she lived there both she and her mother would gang up on Chris calling him names and making fun of him for being gay.

One day while in the city I got a call from one of the tenants that Chris was being beat up by his mother and sister and they had called the police twenty minutes ago and they had not come. As I entered the building, I could hear screaming and Chris crying coming from the third floor where they all lived. I ran up the stairs and found Chris cowered in the corner crying while they taunted him and beat him with mops and brooms. I ordered both of them to stop and they laughed at me. I picked up my cell phone and threatened to call the police and they laughed harder knowing we had little police protection.

"He's a faggot," screamed the mother

"Yeah, he's a faggot "his sister agreed.

"So what, you are a lesbian" I said

"This is your son, this is your brother, what has happened in your life that has made both of you so hateful and so angry? "

It was common knowledge throughout the building that while living there Chris's mother had been in several lesbian relationships. It was not about being gay or lesbian with her and her daughter. It was about being angry causing them to be downright hateful. He was their scapegoat for everything that had gone wrong in their lives. I had complaints prior to this day about them beating on Chris but to see it actually happen was downright sad. With the 2016 election approaching, it was clear who they favored. Hilary Clinton signs had been taped to the walls in their apartment. Their hate towards Chris escalated as hate became a common emotion among the democratic party.

From observation on how people live who harbor feelings of hate and anger, I could see many problems resulting in major frustration. Our success in life is determined by how we deal with the frustrations and many challenges that we personally have. Many people make bad choices, they choose the wrong career, the wrong job, the wrong spouse, or the wrong house with too much debt to name a few. The other things that are stressful and beyond everyone's control will show up in their lives adding to their existing stress. This puts many on a downward spiral they can't recover from placing blame and responsibility somewhere other than on themselves. Over time negative thoughts and feelings are the only thoughts that constantly flood their mind. Attaching these feelings in the form of blame to outside sources may console them temporarily but will cloud any chance of them having ability to identify their problems and prevent them in accepting their personal responsibility. Present day anger was rooted many years ago under failed democratic policies resulting in this anger being passed down to the next generation.

CAUSES OF ANGER

Unemployment

China's entry into the world trade organization stripped every city across America bare of industries leaving thousands of manufacturing workers unemployed. It left in its place much lower paying jobs which seemed to frequently come with reduced hours. This caused many people to work multiple jobs to get forty hours in a week which took additional time away from their families. For many others this meant permanent unemployment living on disability for the rest of a person's career. If jobs ever did come back it would be difficult for those people to be able to transition back into the work force after being out of it for so long.

When manufacturing jobs were very plentiful, many were drawn to those jobs and were employed right out of high school. They found that the rate of pay was much higher than the rate of pay for an entry level of many positions with a college degree. These jobs offered different shifts which were very attractive to women raising a family. Both parents could share in the care of their children eliminating the cost of daycare. When manufacturing moved out of the country, many were left living on unemployment until that ran out. They found that finding another job at anywhere near the pay rate of manufacturing was impossible. If they were in savings or retirement plans at work, those were gone as well. Many were forced to sell their homes and substantially downsize.

Tom and Fran

Tom and Fran had met in high school and were married immediately after. Upon graduation they both got jobs working at different manufacturing companies. They bought their first home in the suburbs. They raised one son working different shifts eliminating day care expense. They paid that house off in full in ten years and moved to a larger home in a nicer area. After paying off the second home in ten years they decided to build a custom home where they would spend the rest of their lives. At that time, they were both thirty-eight years old and had twenty-seven more years to work. They both contributed 12% of their pay towards savings and retirement. The home they built was beautiful with every amenity imaginable, many that they added themselves together on weekends.

Five years later, they both lost those jobs they had worked at for twenty-five years within three months of each other. The stock in the company plummeted leaving them with little savings and no retirement. They were selling their beautiful custom home to live in a trailer located in a trailer park.

As horrible as this story is it was not an uncommon one. This happened to many people, some who had long careers in manufacturing. For people who were near retirement age, the money they had saved in plans at work was gone leaving them to live on social security only. This has left many of those people very angry and financially destitute having to rely on the government to take care of them at the end of their life.

Housing Crisis

There is still much anger surrounding the housing crisis of 2008, which many have never recovered from. The beginning of this crisis were new regulations during the Clinton Administration resulting in loose lending practices and low interest rates under Clinton's Housing and Urban Development Secretary, Andrew Cuomo. Required down payments went from 10% to 3% in 1995 and 0 by the year 2000. In addition, income verification, job verification, bank statements and credit history were no longer a requirement in Clinton's big push to make everyone a homeowner whether they could afford it or not guaranteed by Fannie Mae and Freddy Mac.

I used a Texas Instrument calculator to determine my buyer's mortgage qualification between 1989 and 2000. In 2000 a lender told me not to worry about that but to let my buyers choose the home of their dreams and he would make it work. Many were being qualified on an introductory rate adjustable mortgage which adjusted upward after the introductory period ended. When the Fed raised rates thousands of loans adjusted upward again which caused thousands of loan defaults.

Prior to this many young recently married couples both working full time in manufacturing jobs had goals to save money for a down payment on a home and eventually start a family. From the mid 1980's until 1995 I could count on them staying in my rentals around five years while they saved a 10% down payment and approximately 7% in closing costs as well as each buying a new car and paying it off. They were also required to have three months mortgage payments in the bank that was verified during underwriting. Many were married at around the age of twenty or twenty-one so that would put them at about age twenty-five or twenty-six when they bought their first home and then started their family. They were my best prospects for home buying. Not everyone had these goals and became long term renters which weeded those people out that would have probably been foreclosures in loose lending times.

When manufacturing left Reading and the city was taken over by crime, poverty and drugs the young married people that had lived in the city and got such a great start refused to live there and with no money down lending, purchased homes they couldn't afford or rented suburban rentals that ate up all of their income.

By the year 2000 many people who were qualified for mortgages would not qualify for one of my rentals. I saw instances where it was cheaper for someone to buy a home than rent an apartment. With no money down mortgage programs and closing costs paid by the seller I had tenants who had more money in my rental escrow account than in my real estate sales escrow account. Not knowing what they were getting into because they didn't have to save any money for a down payment, they were unaware that they may need an emergency fund or they should start a home repair fund that they put money into every time they got paid. With new construction homes being built to accommodate the real estate boom many felt that they could alleviate those funds where repairs should not be needed for a few years.

I found that the buyers who had to work hard to save money for down payments were much better informed about real estate. During the five to seven years that they were saving money they were aware of what homes were selling for, the approximate costs of home remodeling and repairs, as well as home furnishings and other things that may be needed. While showing them homes they were always paying attention to the life expectancies on big items such as roofs or heating units. They were very decisive and knew exactly what they wanted. I was able to show them four homes in the morning and have them in an agreement by 5:00pm. Every single buyer I sold a home to during that period of time made an excellent choice and paid a fair price without overpaying. Many never became repeat business for me as they were happy and saw no reason to move again.

The no money down buyers would decide to buy a home impulsively without a plan. They got talked into a home by a real estate agent and overpaid or they looked at many homes having internet access and bought the wrong one. That was just the beginning of many mistakes they made regarding home ownership. They had no idea what repairs would cost and when they found out they panicked having no reserves as lenders required them to have in the past. They were the same people that would file law suits not realizing what attorney's fees would cost them. Because of the fast speed of building new construction homes there were more problems with installation as well as faulty components. This group of people had trouble resolving these problems cost effectively. I lost interest in representing buyers who I felt home buying was not in their best interest. During that time, most of my real estate sales business were listings or buyers who were friends with substantial down payments.

I saw the first wave of foreclosures in 1995 with a few sellers mostly due to manufacturing job losses. Most avoided this by selling their home and substantially downsizing as they realized what was happening to manufacturing. If they had already missed mortgage payments, they had a year before they were legally evicted. The next wave of foreclosures was due to the housing crisis. There were so many that banks did not foreclose immediately but kept many foreclosures on their books taking years to foreclose.

The people who were overextended that came out of the housing crisis without too much damage, were the ones that took immediate action. If they were able to sell breaking even or doing a short sale and moving to cheaper housing, they were able to move on and put the crisis behind them. They were smart enough to realize that even if the economy did turn around, they could not sit in a home that was unaffordable. Others, did not do that but instead sat in a home that financially drained them, leaving them with no extra money to contribute to any savings such as college or retirement funds.

The College Crisis

More young people than ever before are attending college today that would not have when manufacturing jobs were plentiful. They look at attending college as not having any other options rather than training for a field that they would like to work in. This has caused college admission to become more competitive as well as college costs to soar. Because of the shortage of jobs, parents have pushed for admittance to top schools for their children with the mistaken notion that it would give students an edge in the job market. That has caused a lot of anger when parents realized that their rate of return was poor.

Because of the changes in employment today it is more important than ever for young people to explore career options before ever investing the money for education in that field. Young people need to be proactive in discovering career choices that are right for them versus being influenced by someone else. That is what puts many in the wrong career where they may struggle to measure up to the minimum standard leaving them constantly at risk of being terminated.

While working at a waitress job in my late teens I became friendly with a twenty-five-year old married couple who worked as a waiter and a waitress. They were hard working always taking extra hours and had saved a sizeable down payment for a home at the age of twenty-four. Their next goal which they were a year into was paying the house off in seven years. Neither one had ever attended college but had accomplishments that most don't have at their age. One day during a break the husband was asking me about college and my courses. I remember him saying, "do not let your schooling get in the way of your education." What does that mean exactly?

I was told by my parents that education was the ticket to a high paying job and that if I didn't go to college, I would spend the rest of my life in low paying boring jobs with no room for advancement. I now know that is completely false as I have met many people who do not have a college degree and have found much success. I have also met many with college and advanced degrees who are dismal failures. As a small child I watched my father spend evenings going to night school and weekends studying. He was always working on advanced degrees and earned them in both education and engineering. He then went on to work on a PHD in engineering. I was a perceptive enough child to realize that all of his schooling put stress on our family. Even though his employer paid for his education it took time away from his young family while attending his classes as well as the time he spent every weekend studying. At some point my mother demanded an end to his schooling. Any promotions or increases in pay that came to him would have come anyway without advanced degrees that he believed would give him an edge over others. Eventually, the industry my father worked in had major budget cuts which meant layoffs where he worked. It was a disappointment for my parents to find that some of the layoffs included people with lots of education including the highest possible degree of a PHD. It was also very disappointing to those people who lost their jobs that had given so much time and energy to education thinking that it would entitle and guarantee job security.

In the 1950's and 1960's, many companies had not formed a way to measure productivity so they felt that a good place to start was by looking at the credentials in the form of college degrees an applicant had. This left many thinking that having better credentials in the form of degrees entitled them to better paying jobs. It also guaranteed that you could spend a lot of your career performing below standards and continue to receive cost of living raises every year. In the 1970's many companies became aware that experience was very valuable and looked to promote from within if they felt that they had the right person. Companies needed someone who could do the job whether they had a college degree, advanced degree or no degree.

As the economy further expanded in the 1970's a business degree as well as a master's degree in business became what many felt was the ticket to success. My husband had spent most of his career managing people which meant he saw all of their history with the company including promotions, raises, salary information etc. One evening while we were out to dinner with another manager who had all of the same information, they were comparing different employees.

They had two employees who both did the same job at the same rate of pay. One had nothing more than a high school diploma while the other had a master's degree in business. They were talking about how the high school graduate could "run rings" around the highly degreed employee. The employee with the master's degree in business came from a family who had preached that college was a necessity and a master's degree in business was a guarantee for success. Sadly, this employee spent most of his career worrying about being terminated. When the company started measuring performance, he knew he was doomed. Blaming it on the company he left for a similar job at a similar company only to be terminated from there.

As much as I believe that a parent cannot choose their child's field, I have seen some very knowledgeable parents prevent education disasters. I have known some very successful women who rose to great heights in fortune 500 companies with no college education yet going much further than some with a college education. These women started right out of high school in a very entry level position and were promoted many times just by being smart, working hard, and gaining experience along the way. One such woman wanted the college education for her daughter that she had never had herself. Her daughter did not do well her first semester as college was a struggle for her. The mother was smart enough to know that her daughter's performance was a good indication that upon finishing college, the odds were against her of finding a job where college was a requirement as she would be competing with students with much better credentials. The mother recommended that instead of her daughter continuing with college, she should apply for an entry level job at the same company where she worked. It would be a position she would be considered overqualified for if she had a college degree and hurt her chances of getting that job. This is a better choice than finishing college and competing against others who had outperformed her in college. Like her mother, she did very well after demonstrating her driven nature along with good common sense.

Two considerations regarding college today is the cost and the time spent which is time spent out of the workforce. As a real estate broker, I met many college graduates who were unable to afford to buy a home in any area that they were interested in due to time lost in saving for a down payment and a car that they would need to get back and forth to a job. The most common disqualifier for couples were two new car loans. These loans being short terms loans meant increased payments. That alone greatly affected their debt to income ratios and took them out of the housing market. If they enter the job market immediately out of high school and live at home, they can quickly save enough money to pay off a car that they can keep for a number of years as well as accumulate a substantial savings fund for a down payment on a home as well as an emergency fund. I found that many in addition to having student loan debt also had the same income or less than other young people who had immediately entered the job market after high school. This left those people feeling angry leading to the belief that all student loan debt should be forgiven since it left them behind.

The Student Loan Crisis

Student loan debt is a symptom of our housing crisis. When I grew up in the 1970's, it was very common to see every mother go back to work at least part time if not full time to pay for college for her children when those children were in middle school. The children also got jobs in high school working part time after school and weekends as well as full time in the summer to contribute towards their education. Both mothers and their children saved every dollar they made and put that money into a savings account marked solely for college and nothing else.

In the mid to late 1990's I worked on a new construction housing development where many of the customers were second home buyers trading up their first home to meet the needs of their growing families. The typical family was a husband, wife and two or three children. The ages of the children were typically between six and eight which meant that in ten years they would be starting college. Knowing their financial situation to calculate whether they would even qualify for a loan for the home they were interested in, I couldn't possibly see how they would be able to save enough money for college or any part of it with the mortgage payment and property taxes they were about to get into. This meant that in the 1990's, the mother didn't have that advantage of going back to work to save every dollar she made to contribute to college tuition because she was already back at work needing every dollar to maintain the family's lifestyle in that particular house.

Students working and contributing towards their education were generally more responsible and much better at managing their money while in college. They also had a tendency to make better college decisions in terms of cost. For the students who borrowed the entire cost in the form of student loans those decisions were not as good and many times were a disaster.

My first glimpse of this was with a young doctor out of medical school a few years and working for the hospital. He was interested in buying a home I had listed for sale inside of the city limits. The home was in a much lower price range than most doctors would consider. He warned me that his credit score was not good due to "student loan debt." Back in the days before "stated income loans" we needed to know every debt that prospective buyers had including student loan debt as it was factored into their debt to income ratios.

In looking over his information which included bank statements and credit card statements which he considered part of his student loan debt, it became obvious that while in school he lived off credit cards. He also borrowed every dollar for his education. He was single and living with roommates while driving an older car so his rent and car costs were insignificant. In looking over his credit card statements it appeared that he couldn't enter a store without spending $50-$100 each time and there were many of those transactions. His income was not bad but his expenses were out of control. Needless to say, he did not qualify for a mortgage.

My mother, a teacher, told me that another teacher that she worked with and her husband, an attorney, both had student loan debt that they were going to default on because they couldn't afford to pay those loans back. At the opposite end of the spectrum I have seen people who paid off student loan debt in full before ever buying a home. We can argue that was possible because their incomes were higher or their student loan debt was lower but that was not necessarily the case. In many instances they were unable to find jobs in their field and were forced to take much lower paying jobs than the doctor, attorney or teacher in the above examples but still acted responsibly paying that debt in full. They tackled their student loan debt by living in a very cheap rental situation, working two jobs, driving used cars, living on a very tight budget, postponing buying a home or starting a family. They made sacrifices that were sometimes not what they wanted to do but did for a better future. How do you think this group of people would feel if all student loan debt was forgiven?

I also saw parents who did the same thing as the parents did in the 1970's and had no problem paying for their children's college education. They did not buy unaffordable homes, they drove older cars, took cheaper vacations or no vacations, and lived on a budget. How do you think this group would feel if all student loan debt was forgiven?

Even though college costs have substantially increased there are still money saving opportunities for the middle class to go to college. They must first be open to going to a school that will give them the best value for their money. That means giving up the idea of going to an expensive school that they think is prestigious unless they are offering scholarship money for achievement. In those cases, their income does not have to be low to qualify, but if they are exceptional students, they will boost ratings for that school. If not, they will have to pay the entire cost themselves which can be very expensive leaving them with a lot of student loan debt. There is probably a better value somewhere else. Some are under the mistaken notion that certain schools will look good on their resume and open doors for them but today that is not necessarily true. Another very expensive option is for students to go wherever their friends are going. There will rarely be any scholarship options for them in that choice.

Some years back, the Reading Eagle profiled three young women in their early thirties who went back to school to get degrees in teaching and nursing. All three had attended college after high school graduation and dropped out for various reasons. These three women were single moms working full time and attending college at night to get bachelor's degrees to make a better life for themselves and their children. The article showed the entire cost for each of the moms that they were responsible to pay. They were all very cost effective with one starting at community college and then transferring to a local university later where she finished with the courses that she needed to graduate making sure that all credits would transfer. All three of these women were offered jobs in the field that they had pursued immediately upon graduation.

It's worth mentioning that all scholarships are not what they appear to be and much of that depends on the student. Just like schools, scholarships need to be looked at very carefully. One morning I showed a couple a home for sale that they had found advertised online with too much debt to make it saleable. The pictures online made it look much better than it really was and the potential buyers were insistent about seeing the home immediately causing them to take a vacation day from work. The homeowner greeted us at the door and said that she would step out in the yard so we could look at the house. The potential buyers were quickly disappointed and left within a short amount of time. As I turned to leave the seller called me over to ask me if there was any interest with these particular buyers and told me that she was desperate to sell. She and her husband had built the home fifteen years prior using the proceeds from their first home. They were the classic second home buyer with children that would be ready for college in ten years. She was considering getting a job when the kids were in middle school but then between research and advice from friends she decided on a different plan. She found that by not working this would keep her income low enough to qualify for financial aid for college. She also found that more debt would also help. She took out an equity loan on the house which meant another payment and added an addition onto their home which was unnecessary considering their children were at an age where they were close to leaving home. Her daughter had her heart set on a private school and with the financial aid and scholarships she received that school seemed like a good choice. Every year after the first year her aid and scholarships were reduced. The parents used the home equity loan to pay the balance of what was not covered in the remaining years. Their second child was unable to attend college because they ran out of money, so his father got him a job where he had been steadily employed for twenty-five years. Eventually, these people lost their home to foreclosure due to that home equity loan payment being unaffordable.

When choosing a college, all things that may go wrong must be considered so something like this doesn't happen. If a certain grade point average is not maintained students may lose the scholarships and aid that they are receiving. If the school they are attending becomes unaffordable than it was an obvious wrong choice to begin with and a decision must be made. They can transfer to a cheaper school and hope their credits transfer, take out student loans, or leave school altogether and enter the work force or the military. It is the student's responsibility to graduate without incurring extra cost and if they do, then it is their responsibility to pay for it and not their parent's or the tax payers.

School Shootings

For someone to bring a gun to school and start shooting everyone in sight, it's safe to say that there is some serious mental problem with this person that has gone unnoticed. The lack of access to guns does not fix the problem that this person has mentally. The problem is still there and they don't necessarily need a gun to bring harm to someone. What they do need is to be identified as a potential risk so that they can get the help they need before they do bring harm.

Some young people go through a lot of issues while making the transition from a child to an adult. This is a critical period of one's life where they need extra care. Today more than ever there is a lot of lost connection in family's lives. Many children today grow up in single parent families causing the parent with the most responsibility to be out of the home many more hours than they were in the past. Connections between family members are more likely to be broken or not be solidified at all. It is easy to see how a parent in that situation would not be aware of some of the emotions and issues their child is experiencing.

If a student is having problems, he is more likely to tell a friend than a parent, teacher or some other adult. What should a friend do with any questionable information revealed? No one wants to be embarrassed by bringing suspicions to light that turn out to be unfounded. Telling a friend may make someone feel better that they have someone to confide in but if they are having a serious problem, a friend most likely can't help them. The information in some way needs to get to an adult that can help.

Upon entering my junior high school every student was assigned four mandatory appointments with the guidance counselor. There was a man for the boys, and a woman for the girls. I realize now that the purpose was to establish rapport with every student. We were encouraged to talk about anything that was bothering us not only in school, but personal problems we may be having at home. The guidance counselor for the girls, Mrs. Jones, was a woman in her fifties who had raised two children that were grown and married with children of their own. In the opinion of middle school girls, she was really old and square. After the fourth appointment, she had established a rapport with most of the girls and we felt a connectedness to her. We all felt that if we were having a problem, she was someone we could trust and confide in. We were told that if we would like regular appointments with her that we were welcome to make them or if there was anything that came up during the school year that we felt that we needed to talk about she reassured us that she was there for us. She was often seen in the cafeteria eating lunch at a table full of girls. Before long, everyone considered her a respected adult instead of an old and square woman.

I had a lot of friends of all different walks of life in school. Having exposure to a lot of people from different families, I heard a lot of problems that prompted girls especially from troubled families to seek guidance from Mrs. Jones. My friend Joanne had grown up with Debby. They lived in the same neighborhood and knew each other since they were very small. They had played together when they were little, attended nursery school together as well as every school up till the present. Debby was very quiet and had no other friends except for Joanne. One day after gym class, Joanne and I along with another friend were alone in the locker room when Joanne confided in us that Debby was having a problem at home. Debby had confided in Joanne that her older brother had started molesting her over the summer. She did not know what to do and was afraid that if she told her parents, they would not believe her.

Joanne's concern was that she had seen Debby grow very depressed and didn't know what to do. Joanne felt an enormous burden being the only one that knew and I believe wanted some suggestions from me and another friend, two trusting friends, as to how she could help her friend. This is an example of a problem that is too big for a kid to handle. We came up with an idea that Joanne would talk to Debby and convince her to tell Mrs. Jones. We thought it best if Debby did not know that we knew and that Joanne could offer to go with her on the appointment.

If there was no Mrs. Jones, this problem would have gone on and only gotten worse. Problems like this have the potential to escalate with the victim taking out the rage they feel on innocent victims. I don't know what ever happened to this idea of counseling for personal problems being available to students at school. Instead, it seems that guidance counselors are more focused on academics, scholarships, and helping students get acceptances to colleges. This all becomes secondary to the wellness of students and preserving their lives.

To implement a guidance system successfully that will help students with highly sensitive personal problems trust must first be established between the student and the counselor. This takes a very special person who has the ability to connect with young students that feel comfortable enough to talk about these issues. This is difficult considering that the age of these students is a very awkward one. Instead of our public schools spending money on worthless programs, I believe a guidance program like what was available at my junior high would be money well worth spent and could possibly save lives. The situation with Debby results in feelings of isolation, depression and rage to name a few. These are the same feelings which fuel many school shootings.

19

RACISM

July 1968

I was very excited about going to overnight Girl Scout camp for two weeks. It sounded like so much fun with activities during the day and then sleeping in wooden structures they referred to as tents. There were hundreds of girls from all over the state with different camp sites separating me from anyone I knew from my troop. When we ate meals in the large pavilion, I knew no one as we were assigned to eat at different times. Tents had six single beds and there were six girls assigned to each tent.

My tent consisted of four white girls from an upper-class white neighborhood and one black girl, Charlene, from the inner city and me from a middle-class neighborhood. The four white girls were close friends from the same troop and quickly chose the four beds together at the front of the tent. My bed and Charlene's were together at the back of the tent. The girls were very absorbed in their own conversations since they knew each other so well and Charlene and I were left out. An overwhelming feeling of loneliness and exclusion came over me and got worse day by day. At night the girls would talk amongst themselves while Charlene and I were silent. By the third night they started telling racist jokes.

At eleven years old I did not know what racism was. My parents didn't tell those jokes and neither did their friends or my friends. Before one of the girls would tell a joke, they would say, "oh by the way Charlene, don't take offense by this." I was feeling very uncomfortable about the jokes while at the same time dealing with other feelings of homesickness. By the second night of the racists jokes after everyone fell asleep, I heard Charlene crying softly in her bed. On the third night when one of the girls said "oh by the way Charlene, don't take offense by this" and she said what she usually said, "I know, its ok", I said, "I don't think it is ok with Charlene and its not ok with me either so let's not tell those jokes." Everyone fell silent. The four girls never talked to me or Charlene again and shortly after we were both moved to other tents.

Racial Riots

1975

As I drove up to my high school and parked, something didn't seem right. It was unusually quiet and very few students were seen walking across campus as well as hanging out in the archways. A student ran up to my car and motioned for me to wind my window down.

"The black students are rioting inside of the school and teachers have locked themselves and some others into the classroom. They will be outside in a few minutes looking to kill anyone who is white, get out and get out now, you are not safe" he said in a voice filled with panic.

As cars pulled up with white students, he delivered the same message to each of them. This was the third racial riot on the campus where I attended high school and there had been others before I got there. There had been injuries and casualties on campus to students who just happened to be in the wrong place at the wrong time and not involved in the cause of it. The school had an excellent reputation academically but was not safe because of the racial tension that existed before and during the time I attended high school there. These problems were not publicized so were unknown to parents until their children arrived on campus. Many parents who could afford to, enrolled their children in all white private schools.

Racial tension in the 1960's and 1970's broke out in inner cities where much of the protest was for better housing in urban areas, less crime, and the drafting of the poorest to be shipped off to Vietnam. It was a national problem that existed across the nation which I had been exposed to in two different areas. Where I was born and raised in Connecticut, I felt the tension as it was common to hear about racial riots breaking out in the north end of Hartford, Connecticut in the 1960's. While I was living in Connecticut, blacks and whites did not live in the same neighborhoods or attend the same schools and churches. The only time when black and white people came together was shopping areas which were located in cities.

When my father took a new job in New Jersey, attending school with black students was a new experience for me. The hate was stronger than ever as black students took over an area of the school right outside of the principal's office. It was well known that you did not walk anywhere near there or enter the school at that entrance if you were white. This rule was set up by the black students that occupied that entrance. My mother and I did not know that when we went to register me for school. We were both intimidated as we were stared down while a black male student swung two feet of chain as we walked by. When my mother mentioned this to the administration, they told us to avoid that entrance.

These were ground rules set up by black students in protest of being bused from the inner city of Trenton. Tension escalated when white students made remarks to black students that were offensive. Black students designated certain tables in the cafeteria and certain areas of the school which were off limits to white students. If anyone stood up to them it would spark rioting and violence. White students separated white students by our personalities. Our high school was an old building with arches at the entryways and we were assigned entryways as well as names of who they decided we were. For the white people the names assigned were, the jocks, the druggies, the greasers, and the sluts and fags. Not hanging out in your proper place could spark violence.

This was something that existed long before I ever arrived at the school. Teachers and administration had no control over it and if they tried to intervene, a riot erupted. The police patrolled the outskirts of the school all day in patrol cars but did not walk on campus. In the fall of my sophomore year of high school I turned sixteen years old and got a job after school. I arranged all of my classes in the morning and left school at lunchtime to go to my part time job.

On the other side of Route #1 where I lived, Princeton Junction, was a predominantly white suburban neighborhood that had recently developed from farmland to housing developments to house the relocations moving into those neighborhoods to work at fortune 500 companies in the area, Many had originally been located in New York City and had moved out of the area for better commercial leasing opportunities. Some of the people still worked in the city which was an easy commute from the train station located in Princeton Junction.

A new high school was built in Princeton Junction to educate just those students living there. I was the last graduating class at Princeton High School that lived in Princeton Junction. For those of us who lived in Princeton Junction, we had our own group of friends who shared the same neighborhoods. Many of us hung out after school at a nearby elementary school with a playground off of the parking lot.

Tyrone was a black student who went to school with us but lived in Princeton Junction. His mother had married a white man and they lived in a beautiful home in that area. Every so often he would show up at the school in Princeton Junction where we hung out after school and weekends. One evening as I drove into the parking lot, I found Tyrone sitting on a park bench by himself. I went over and sat down on the same park bench as that was ok since we were far away from our high school campus. We began to talk about the racial problems at our high school. Tyrone said that the protests were over busing. Black students were angry about being bused to a school district where they did not want to attend school but would prefer to stay in their own public school. He told me he had nothing against white people but would rather not live or go to school with them. He did not like the large beautiful house where he lived in the suburbs and said that he felt out of place. He said, "I want to live with my own people." I was not insulted by that because I believe I was able to have empathy after my girl scout camp experience. I knew what it felt like to feel exclusion and to feel as though I didn't fit. I would never force circumstances on people that would make them feel that way.

August 2015

A white new Toyota slowly glided down the street, and came to a stop below the window in the apartment where I was inspecting an apartment for a move in the next day. The traffic below this particular window went on like this all hours every day. I knew that the driver of the car was either looking for a prostitute or looking to buy drugs or both.

As I was finishing up the last of the inspection, I heard a loud crash below. I looked out the window but was unable to see the part of the street where there seemed to have been a car accident. Walking down the stairs and out the front door the same white Toyota had hit a van while pulling out onto the main road. The occupants of the van were inspecting the damage while the man in the Toyota continued to sit in his car. They were Hispanic and spoke no English, dressed as though they had just come from church. I remembered that it was Sunday. A crowd gathered in the block and watched as the man in the Toyota got out of his car and started stumbling. He was obviously incoherent and under the influence of something. He got back into his car and floored the gas while the car was in reverse. He plowed into the stop sign as the car jumped the curb. By this time 30-40 people were in the street laughing, clapping and cheering. He got out of the car and yelled "what are all of you niggers laughing at." I had not heard that word since high school. I realized at that moment that the driver and me were the only white people standing on the block of a predominantly black neighborhood.

1974

As I sat in my friend's car with a few other friends, we watched as school bus after school bus sat at the crossroad at the corner of our high school. We watched as at least 100 black students from Trenton got off the buses and marched in single file towards the front doors of the school. I felt sheer panic as law enforcement was powerless to do anything. It was not the first time this had happened and would not be the last.

August 2015

We had come so far that I had not looked at color in years. Vivid flashbacks of my high school and the violence that I hadn't thought about in years flooded my mind. I ran over to the car looking into the passenger side at the driver sitting at the wheel and said "are you crazy, you want to get us killed, what is the matter with you". No one was reacting the way they would have reacted during racial tension of the 1960's and 1970's. Instead the 30-40 black people on the block laughed, cheered and clapped. These were young people who were unaware of that racial divide so long ago because they had not been born yet.

Someone in the crowd asked a Hispanic man to go talk with the couple that stood helplessly in the middle of the street with a van that was not drivable. Someone reached into the white Toyota and grabbed the keys out of the ignition. I asked the crowd if someone had called the police. The crowd laughed at my question. The tall black girl with dreadlocks towered over me as she said, "Miss Marilyn, you must be high on the same thing that dude is. No cops are coming down to this block." The crowd laughed some more. I said to her "This dude cannot leave the block unescorted." A number of people had called. One of my tenants was just walking into the block from being out somewhere. She had spent a good part of her life in prison for prostitution and drug dealing but was presently in treatment. I asked her if she knew the guy and she admitted that he was not a regular but did come down looking for drugs and a prostitute occasionally. His car had a sticker on the back from a dealership in Chester County. He was very clean looking sporting a neatly pressed button-down shirt and khaki pants, not a common look on this block. Two Mexican men circled the new white Toyota as the intoxicated driver kept waiving them away.

Just around the time that everyone gave up on the police, three showed up in two squad cars. While one police officer helped the Hispanic couple, the other two had the driver of the white Toyota get out of the car and try to walk a straight line. While their backs were turned the Mexican men again circled the Toyota and grabbed something through the windows of the car, throwing it in the bushes. The police escorted the man into a patrol car and a tow truck arrived to tow his car. The police left and the crowd thinned. The Mexican drug dealers reached into the bushes taking whatever drugs they had thrown there to resell on the street.

Manipulating Racism

In addition to working in the inner city with rentals I also sold homes as a real estate broker in the surrounding suburban areas. Katharine and John lived in a lovely suburban neighborhood and wanted to sell their home. After listing their home for sale, they requested that I postpone showings so they could have additional time to make the improvements I had recommended. For the next several weeks we spoke frequently and had a great rapport and then suddenly that changed. Speaking mostly with Katharine I had a feeling that something was very wrong. As we prepared to put the pictures of the home in multi list, Katharine said that she had second thoughts about the pictures of her home. I had a feeling that something else was wrong and kept asking questions.

When I asked what specifically was wrong with the photos, she said that they made her home look like a "city row home." Katharine told me that I was an urban kind of realtor serving an urban kind of community which makes me the wrong person to market their home. One of my marketing pieces that John and Katharine were given the day I listed their home was a "Homes Sold" list showing many homes that I sold over the years all over the county and including their area. More were sold in the suburbs than in the "urban area" that she was referring to. That marketing piece alone should have given them all the information they needed as to whether I was the right realtor or not. Also, in my marketing material was information about me including my years as a property manager in the city. If that bothered them it should have bothered them when they first saw that and not six weeks later.

When they spoke to other people about the fact that they listed their home, another realtor with very little experience put that idea in their head in attempt to get them to withdraw their listing with me so that he could list it. Since he had few homes sold and little experience, he had no marketing platform but to undermine me by telling these people that the pictures were not good and I'm an "urban realtor" and therefore not fit to list their home. Labeling people or assigning them to a group can be very offensive which I don't think these people meant for it to be offensive but it is. This is why educating people is so important. For sellers to actually give this person any attention indicates that they have little self-confidence and few life experiences to be able to make decisions independently of other's opinions. People like this will drain your energy and time needing constant explanations for others opinions which is why I gave them back their listing so that I could maintain my sanity.

In looking at the four girls from girl scout camp and Katharine and John, these are examples of people from upper class all white neighborhoods who lack an understanding of diversity and inclusion. This is a result of having little contact with people of diverse backgrounds. This demographic group was targeted heavily for education in diversity. My high school being located over on the other side of the highway fit that profile. They bused many students from the inner city to my high school that didn't want to be there in the first place. In this instance, busing students from the poorest districts to the wealthiest did not accomplish what it was intended to do.

In more recent years, wealthy white school districts needing diversity education have brought people of diverse backgrounds in to teach those classes. We need to be very careful that those teachers are sincere and genuine and not teaching radical terrorist ideas. During the time I spent in high school my parents would not have wanted the Symbionese Liberation Army teaching what they claim to be diversity. When teachers promote rioting, violence, setting buildings on fire or burning the American flag they could be promoting terrorism and worse yet, recruiting students for their cause. If teachers like this infiltrate our school systems instead of kidnapping people such as what happened to Patty Hearst in the mid 1970's, no alarm bells go off. When they teach in our schools, they have access to our children without their parents and the administration realizing what the students are being taught. Parents trust schools to make good decisions while hiring mistakes do happen.

In the city of Reading we had gang related murders with black, white and Hispanic people being murdered by people in this country illegally. We had bonded together wanting safer streets for all of us, black, white, and Hispanic Americans. Groups from out of town came into our town pushing an agenda that white people are racists when Donald Trump first announced he was running for president back in 2015. This is the first step in creating division which paves the way to racism. This promotes division and violence instead of unity and unity is what Donald Trump is trying to promote here in our country.

The media's reporting on the death of George Floyd sparked outrage causing racial tension bringing forth the rioting and violence we have seen recently. On June 1, 2020 I would see all of my tenants to collect rent, a mixture of white, black and Hispanic people. The racial tension caused me to think about which tenants were black and would they look at me differently. Would we be back to the racial tension I lived with at my high school in the 1970's. It sure sounded like we were headed that way. In my mind, there are two types of people, those who have bad characteristics such as anger, hatred, and negativity, and positive people whose characteristics are the opposite of that. I chose the people with good characteristics never thinking about their color until that day. I found that I had an equal mix of black, white and Hispanic tenants. Forcing people to think about what color people are creates division, and then causes people to separate themselves into groups like what happened in my high school. This is extremely destructive to society as a whole.

When a political party has no big picture in mind of what needs to be done and no plan on how to do it, the only thing they can do is come up with false information such as what happened to me with Katharine and John. Those sellers needed to act more responsibly and go back and review all my marketing materials including the detailed plan to sell their home instead of listening to someone assigning labels.

If we want to be part of the solution to racism, we can extend a hand to each other. I think that is better than just talking about it. The person who taught me this set a tremendous example of it back in 1978 without knowing me or that he set that example. That person was Donald J. Trump himself.

December 1978 -Making Christmas Great Again

I was working for a pharmaceutical company and helping out with the scheduling of limo drivers for their executives which were contracted through a private limo company. Most of the scheduling was set up in the lobby at a very large circular reception desk where the drivers would come in and stand around the desk waiting for their assignments. They worked for other businesses as well and I found it very informative to listen to the stories of many highly successful people that the limo drivers drove.

A month before Christmas they hired Louis, a black man around age forty, who had spent most of his life as either a taxi driver or limo driver. He was thrilled to get the job as hard times had fallen on him. He had lost his job a year before due to his previous employer going out of business. His wife had been diagnosed with cancer and was treating while they were raising two children under the age of ten. As much as he had gone through some hard times, he came into work every day with a positive attitude. He mentioned that it would be a very sparse Christmas as he was just getting back on his feet after being out of work for a year.

Two days before Christmas, late in the afternoon, the drivers came in to pick up the executives and bring them home. I noticed Louis standing near the very tall

Christmas tree that stood in a corner of the lobby away from everyone. The lights were dimmed in the lobby and the miniature Christmas lights on the tree shone brightly. In the light, I noticed a tear rolling down Louis's cheek. I was sure that something had gone wrong with his wife and her treatment. When everyone wandered out, I walked over to Louis and noticed that it wasn't just one tear but many.

He told me that the most incredible thing had happened that day. He had been assigned to go to New York and drive Donald Trump around for the day. That wasn't anything unusual as Donald Trump was known to use limo services. He was also known to be very personable so it was not unusual for him to talk to the drivers. The story came out about the hardships that Louis and his family had been through and how grateful he felt that the limo service had hired him. I'm sure Donald Trump saw this as an opportunity to make Louis' Christmas great. He had Louis drive up to a department store in New York where he bought the family Christmas presents as well as winter coats for each child. They were all wrapped in the back of the limo and ready for Louis to take home to give to his family. I will never forget what Louis said to me right there at that moment in time through his tears. "I have spent all of my adult life driving a lot of very wealthy white men but never have I met one like Donald Trump. Don't get me wrong, they were very nice but many white folks would never extend a hand over that line that divides whites and blacks and show kindness to people of color."

I had graduated from my high school with racial tension three years before and knew all too well what an incredible act of kindness this was. The problems between blacks and whites were still unresolved which made this act so unusual during that time. I believe that Donald Trump did not extend this kindness because he felt sorry for Louis and regarded him as a poor black man but instead, regarded Louis as a family man who had some struggles but was out there every day working and trying to lift his family up through hard times. Business people who work hard know what hard work is and have no problem extending a hand to someone who is giving his work his best effort with a positive attitude.

As I write this in the year 2020, I think everyone that grew up in racially tense times will admit that we have come a long way. The people who are younger and have not had that experience could not possibly know the hatred and destruction that follows and takes years to mend. We have come a very long way in this country from what I lived with personally in the 1960's and 1970's. We cannot afford to regress back to those horrific times and for groups of people to try to bring those times back to gain power is very destructive to our society and what we have worked towards for so long.

Through sales and property management I have met many people and have had many conversations with those people that often drifted off of the subject of real estate and onto other matters. These conversations gave me great insight on how people think and what causes them to have the perceptions they have. This is extremely educational if the people we interact with are from diverse backgrounds versus people who are exactly like us. People who talk to the same dozen people or so who are exactly like them have a tendency to be intolerant to anyone who differs from them. They are even more intolerant if their information comes from limited sources.

Students are taught from a text book with one slanted point of view which they attach to because of lack of life experiences. In the 1970's different cult groups recruited these students on college campuses because they were so easily brainwashed in comparison to someone growing up with many different life experiences. Studies found that the most successful recruits were students from upper class white backgrounds. Many of their parents hired deprogramming services to try to deprogram brainwashed victims who refused to leave the cults that had hijacked them mentally.

The media represents a handful of reporters with one viewpoint that many will attach themselves to because of their limited life experiences. I recently read an article stating that black people are more likely to be pulled over than white people by the police during routine traffic stops but yet a black couple in their late forties told me that they had never been stopped by the police. I asked many people of diverse backgrounds how many times they were pulled over by the police during routine traffic stops and not one has been able to come anywhere near my record of several dozen times. In addition, I have been detained and patted down in airports three times while I watched people of diverse backgrounds go through. Because of those life experiences it would be unlikely that the media would be able to convince me that black people are pulled over by the police more than white people. However, if I was a person who had been pulled over just a few times or none at all, there would be a much higher probability that I would believe that article. I probably have been pulled over more because of the amount of time I'm on the road in comparison to most. I also probably travel more than most.

In all of the times that I have been pulled over, they were for reasons such as, a brake light was out, a head light was out, twice for speeding, driving over the line in the road to name a few. I owe it to my father who told me how to handle being pulled over by the police resulting in those episodes being uneventful. Hopefully what he told me all those years ago, could be helpful to others.

First, put yourself in the place of the police officer pulling you over. Even though he has quickly run your license plate, he doesn't know who is driving the car. You could be crazy with mental illness, under the influence, or your car could have been stolen and a crazed madman could be behind the wheel. The best thing you can do is put the police officer at ease and smile with a greeting when he approaches. I've seen the stress disappear from police officer's faces when I did this. Have your driver's license, registration, and insurance card always in the same places so you can

281

have it immediately available if he asks for it. Don't demand to know why you were pulled over, they will tell you soon enough. Never have an attitude and never argue with the police officer. If he gives you a ticket, you will have your day in court if you feel you are not guilty. If you are guilty, check the guilty box, send in the fine, and let it be a lesson.

Police are not the enemy they are here to enforce the law and keep us safe. It is their job to stop people if something doesn't seem right. While driving in a bad area of the city, I turned left in the left lane of a busy one-way street. My turn was too wide cutting off a police car who was also turning left in the right lane. He immediately pulled me over. As he approached my car, I wound down my window and said,

"Officer, I am so sorry, I can't believe that I just cut you off. It was an accident and I apologize." He looked at me suspiciously. I saw his eyes dart around the inside of my car. I sat back in my seat so that he could get a better look.

"Are you alright?" he asked

"I'm fine"?

"That is what is most important, that you are alright, have a good day."

Driving under the influence today is more common that ever due to the drug epidemic. This police officer pulled me over because he was doing his job. If I was under the influence, he would have called for backup, and removed me from my car so that I don't floor the gas and lead them on a chase putting others in harm's way. If he had decided not to do his job, or didn't do it right, and I had been under the influence, I could have killed your child, your spouse, your brother or sister, your mother or father or someone else that means a lot to you.

20

WHAT MAKES A LEADER

As a child, I often had the same reoccurring nightmare. I would wake up in the tiny cape cod home where we lived and find that everyone had left. My parent's car was in the driveway as well as all of the other neighbor's cars but no one was at home. I would walk down the street and turn the corner to the next street and would find the same thing, everyone gone on every street. I would sob uncontrollably realizing that I was the only person left. How would I survive in a world without people? We depend on people to take care of us when we are sick, to grow food that we eat, to supply energy to our homes, to work in manufacturing jobs that supply the goods that we buy and leaders to lead us, to name a few things. It would take me a few days to recover from having that nightmare as I had a lingering sick feeling. Little did I know at the time that I would grow up one day to live that nightmare.

I watched a great manufacturing city turn into a hellish nightmare in slow motion and as I watched, I had that same lingering sick feeling that I had in my dream. In the 1980's to the early 1990's no matter what neighborhood from the inner city to the most expensive, people had pride. Lawns were perfectly manicured as well as landscaping. The insides of the homes I saw on real estate office tours at that time were very clean and well decorated with just a little money spent. My mother often remarked when visiting, that every neighbor up and down the street kept their properties in excellent condition. This was the result of the citizens choosing a town to live in that offered a reasonable cost of living with an abundance of job opportunities. It was a great place to raise a family as many children were being raised by their parents who were not caught in the frenzy of needing two incomes to survive. This resulted in more time spent with children so that they were sent to school ready to learn while parents continued to be involved in their education. That means better schools with better results. It also means lower school taxes when many extra programs and extra administration are not needed by the students.

Cities and towns across our country where manufacturing jobs were once abundant, slowly over decades left those cities and towns unrecognizable to many older folks. Younger people didn't notice the difference as that was all they ever knew. Bad leadership causes many great citizens who add value to a community, to look for better opportunities in other cities and towns.

In the late 1970's I worked for an attorney in New Jersey whose office was located across the street from the courthouse where we routinely filed documents. Even though their hours were from 8:30am to 4:00pm the only time you were able to get service was between 10:00am and 11:30am or 2:00pm and 3:30pm. Employees routinely came into work very late, took long lunch hours, and left early. The best times to go over to the courthouse for service was 10:00am or 3:20pm when the line was the shortest. One day, I went over at 3:15pm and one person was practicing to go on the Gong Show while everyone else acted as the audience. They told me they were closed for the day and that I would have to come back the next day. It was a known fact that any government/state job was very low paying in comparison to working in the private sector. The advantages were good benefits, more paid holidays and vacation time, more paid sick time and it was impossible to be terminated. This attracts the most unproductive workers who care more about working as little as possible than being challenged to achieve excellence. No matter how unproductive they are, as long as they put in their time they are often promoted and many to leadership roles where they don't belong. When there is no leadership in a department such as the courthouse situation I have described, very little gets accomplished.

In dealing with different government offices and employees, I found the same level of below average performance. In writing letters to different heads of city government dealing with problems in the city of Reading every letter went unanswered. If there was a problem that I was bringing attention to, it was ignored. For elected officials, the problem is worse. These are people who have decided to run for an office because they believe the job is much easier than working in a business and they get healthcare provided to them. That may be true if they face no challenges but when they do, they have no experience in handling them and can make terrible choices or no choices at all. Under this leadership, the problems that have existed in our cities for decades have little chance of being fixed.

Many people feel that it is not their concern if they don't live there and believe that anyone who is bothered by it should just move. That doesn't solve any problems that eventually permeate into the surrounding areas. The problem lies in the lack of awareness that inner city problems will affect all Americans eventually leaving them in a society that is unsafe.

Cities reached a low point after the housing crisis leaving many buildings vacant to house people in this country illegally. Vacant industrial buildings once used for manufacturing were used to prepare shipments of illegal drugs for sale on the street. Businesses that once thrived that sold services or goods to manufacturing companies were gone leaving buildings vacant after owners had no recourse but to file for bankruptcy. My own business providing housing, never suffered an economic downturn because people always need housing. If they can't pay for it, the government will. So why should I care? I cared very much for the people, the people who earned $25 an hour twenty-five years ago. That is $4000 a month instead of the $750 in disability they were forced to live on after the market crash of 2009. I remember a time when I had set up laundry rooms with pinball machines and vending machines where people could do laundry, play a game and have a snack while they waited. Living on disability income they can't afford to do laundry and definitely can't afford to play pinball machines or buy a snack. I shut those rooms down not creating a hardship for me because it wasn't the major income generator for my business. However, there were buildings purchased in Reading that served as game rooms where owners had to give them back to the bank or declare bankruptcy. There were many examples of small businesses that couldn't survive after manufacturing left. I had given up hope of ever seeing any resolutions for the inner cities in this country. Day after day since 2009 I had that sick feeling that I had as a child when I woke up from my reoccurring nightmare. My dream was very symbolic of what had happened in our country as many did not have a true awareness that something needed to be done. The frustration that I often felt reminded me of a horror movie from the 1970's known as the Stepford Wives. The setting for the movie was in a flawed community known as Stepford where the residents were unable to see their town's flaws as they sunk deeper into them where they were eventually destroyed.

Donald Trump addressed our failing cities in his speech in Charlotte, NC on October 26, 2016 with his plan on urban renewal and rebuilding our cities. He acknowledged that some of our inner cities are more dangerous than war zones that we hear about. His solution would be to empower cities and states to seek a federal disaster designation for blighted communities, to demolish abandoned properties, rebuild vital infrastructure and to increase law enforcement. He spoke about his immigration policy being one that would restore the civil rights of African Americans,

Hispanics as well as all Americans by ending illegal immigration through building a wall. His wall would greatly reduce the massive inflow of drugs that pour into our country killing so many of our own citizens. He would reform visa rules to give the American worker preference for jobs and suspend refuge admissions from regions that cost tax payers hundreds of billions of dollars. He spoke about China's entry into the World Trade Organization and the trade deals that stripped towns like Reading, PA of manufacturing costing many Americans jobs. NAFTA a failed democratic economic policy needed to be renegotiated. Obviously since it wasn't in the past no one had the skill to do that before costing our country billions of dollars and the American worker's jobs. Donald Trump has a long history of success in many of his real estate projects. He didn't get there without negotiation skills.

When he spoke about these problems and solutions it was obvious that he had really visited and talked with the citizens of some failed cities as he said he did. This is the first step in solving problems is being aware that they exist and understanding how they occurred. Many politicians promise great things campaigning, but it is up to us to ask ourselves if they can really deliver on their promises. A good way to determine that is to look at their background, their experience and their past successes.

Donald Trump had started in his father's business dealing in rental housing as well as construction of new housing. With that experience it would be likely that he would be familiar with issues in inner cities more so than most other politicians. When manufacturing moved out of my own area, the city of Reading was greatly affected becoming the "missing link" to real estate sales in every price range. Real estate sales depended on the inner city, the beginning of the link of a chain of homes selling and without it, home values stagnate or decrease.

Every politician before Donald Trump has admitted that undocumented people living in the United States is a problem but offered no solutions to stop it. They also acknowledged that human trafficking involving children is a problem and took measures to stop it by detaining children at the border. Many children are brought to this country and trafficked by their own parents. They are much safer in their own country versus the United States where pedophiles have the financial means to pay for them. Building a wall provides many benefits including safety for children.

During the 2016 election it was very obvious to me who the American public's choice was. As I drove through neighborhoods in all price ranges, I saw many signs supporting Donald Trump and very few supporting Hilary Clinton. Trump's speech in North Carolina in October 2016 addressed the vast problems that cities had faced for decades because of failed democratic policies and he had a plan to fix them. It wasn't a surprise that he had the support of more of the black and Hispanic population in the inner cities than many people realized.

My mother would never discuss how she really felt with anyone that may provoke a confrontation and would say anything she had to say to avoid it. She knew that she could always talk to me as we did share very similar view points on many issues. I considered my mother to be a person with a great deal of common sense so when she confided in me that she was uncertain who to vote for in the 2016 election I was surprised.

At the time, being in her eighties, she had outlived my father as well as many of her friends so the only reference she had was the media. She thought that the media told the truth because that would be the right thing to do. She became confused after seeing Ivanka Trump interviewed on a talk show where they asked her why the media said such bad things about her father. Ivanka Trump said that she didn't understand why they said terrible things about her father because he was one of the nicest kindest human beings and had done so much for so many people. My mother said to me, "you know, I thought she was such a lovely young woman and I'm confused as to how her father, being as bad as the media paints him, could have raised such a lovely daughter."

The memory of that Christmas back in the late 1970's when Donald Trump bought an entire family Christmas presents immediately flooded my mind. There were so many good stories about him that the media never reported. At the time, he had no intention of running for president and it was so far back in the past. It demonstrates what kind of a person he truly is when no one is paying attention. I have never met Donald Trump personally but growing up in New

Jersey I was the recipient of one of his acts of kindness as I'm sure many have been.

March 1979

As I slid into the limousine with my father on the day of my wedding, the limo driver turned to my father and said,

"you will never believe who just sat where you are sitting now"

"Who is that?" asked my father

"Donald Trump"

"where did you drive him"

"I picked him up in New York and drove him and another guy to Atlantic City"

"Why did he go there"

"I think from the conversation he may be considering investing in Atlantic City"

I thought to myself how incredible it would be if he were actually considering development in Atlantic City. He seemed like the only solution to turn that city around and give it some hope. When I thought of his projects that brought much improvement to areas in New York City, this was proof enough that he was the answer to a lot of what was needed to make that city a resort that people would vacation at.

The driver continued the conversation about Donald Trump as we drove to the church where I was to be married at 4:00pm that day. Donald Trump had asked the driver if he could hang around Atlantic City and drive him back to New York later. When the driver told him that he had to be back in Princeton for a wedding, Donald Trump turned to the driver as he slid out of the limo and said,

"I'm certainly not going to interfere in such an important event as that."

The driver thought that was incredibly generous of him. He told us that it was difficult sometimes to deal with wealthy people as many would have insisted that they are a better customer and that the limo service should find someone else to transport a bride. If he had done that it would have presented a problem as they were short staffed that day due to illness of one of the drivers.

Those American people who have been close enough to know the truth are the people you will see at his rallies cheering him on and touting signs that read, "Blacks for Trump", "Women for Trump", "Gays for Trump", and "Lesbians like Trump", You will not see them on TV because the media will always turn the cameras away from those groups only showing a predominately white crowd that they would imply were racists.

This discussion with my mother helped me to understand that everyone has had different life experiences that cause them to make different choices. Everyone is entitled to accurate reporting from the media but since that is not what is happening citizens need to do their own research. For people like me who have been close enough to see what Donald Trump is really like, the media lost all credibility from the beginning.

Needless to say, it takes more than a good kind person to be a leader. The best leaders have visions of the future and what it will look like long after they have departed. Their objective is to leave this life much better than when they entered, therefore, they must give up themselves. It is not "what's in it for me", but what's in it for many more generations to come. With that objective, a true leader has a definite plan of what is to be accomplished and how they will do it. We look to leaders in tough times to give us hope by staying strong and continuing to have a plan when times become challenging and making good decisions for us. A leader must be in good health with excellent cognitive ability to be able to accomplish great things. Good leadership starts at the top and filters down. When poor leadership is in place, we have everyone below working like the courthouse workers that I have described, believing that is the norm. We have needed someone with business skills to run this country for a long time.

October 2016

As more and more undocumented people poured into the city, the problems they brought with them continued to escalate. The state workers assigned to address those problems seemed to zone out. Whether I was fighting for the protection of a child, help from the codes department for the excess trash dumped on my property, help from the police department who felt it too dangerous to come down to some neighborhoods to do their job or any of the numerous other problems I dealt with on a daily basis I felt that everyone had fallen asleep behind the wheel. I feared for the safety of our country as I had visions of the gang violence over drugs caused by open borders erupting minutes from where I live. I knew that if it is not stopped soon it will continue to expand until it swallows our country. We desperately needed powerful and aggressive leadership with a real understanding and actual awareness of the dangerous direction our country was headed in. We were now at the 11th hour of the problems with the election being just weeks away. Later at lunchtime I said to my son,

"we are all screwed if the Donald loses"

"he's not losing"

"the media says Hilary is ahead"

"it's wrong, I have traveled across the country in August on my golf trip traveling north and then south and I saw no signs for Hilary, but massive "Trump for president signs.""

"why are they reporting that she is ahead"

"I don't understand why it is being reported that way. Traveling across the country I saw something very different than what is being reported by the media, I would be shocked if Trump doesn't win."

From the street view it was very obvious who the American people wanted as their next president. My fear was that the 2016 election would be stolen and the American people would not get their choice. The day of the election I knew it was our last chance to get our country back on track. If we lost that chance our country would continue on the same dark path it had already been on. I dozed off with the news on, I could not fall asleep until I heard the result. When they announced that Donald Trump had won, I fell into a deep peaceful sleep. I had not slept that well in years.

Donald Trump has fought for the American worker and has put America first since he took office in 2016. He has not taken large campaign donations from businesses in exchange for favors which so many of those businesses have become wealthy on and depend on. Any money that was given to businesses during the pandemic was for the sole purpose of keeping the American worker employed.

December 2016

Within a month of Donald Trump winning the election, I saw change in the street on one of the worst blocks in the city. The prostitution trade became almost nonexistent as the heroin trade was dramatically reduced. The most violent criminals disappeared and stabbings and shootings slowed down. Donald Trump hadn't taken office yet and already there was change occurring because of the promise of law enforcement by a leader who really meant it. Many on the block who were in this country illegally left the country without having to be deported. I entered the building in that neighborhood and climbed the stairs to a second-floor vacant apartment. I looked out the window to see a police car pull up and stop instead of just doing a drive by. I was surprised because the criminals had all left the block. The only people left that the police could be coming for were those with unpaid traffic or parking fines. When they lock tenants up for unpaid fines, they are then unable to pay rent. Their families needed them at home but the city needed the money. I heard the door open across the hall and my tenant walked out of his apartment and down the hall. I followed him down the hall and called out to him as he continued to walk down the stairs.

"Hey, do you hear what I'm saying to you."

No response.

"I'm telling you the cops are out front"

No response.

"Are they looking for you?"

As he got to the front door to exit the building, he threw back his head and laughed while he yelled over his shoulder,

"not today!"

ACKNOWLEDGEMENTS

As my cousin and I watched the Watergate hearings on national television in the summer of 1973, we wondered exactly what the perception and thoughts of the American people were. We compiled a list of questions regarding the scandal and went to a supermarket blocks from my house and interviewed people recording those conversations as they came out of the store. When we played the recorder back and listened to those interviews, we realized that this represented one segment of the population. The next day and the day after, we went to other areas and asked the same questions. I believe we ended up with around fifty interviews representing people of different races, religions and socio-economic backgrounds.

The more people we talk to, the more we learn. Our prospective is broadened and our eyes opened to things we know little about. From that day forward, I have asked many questions and accumulated a vast amount of information. Therefore, I would like to recognize all of those people who made it possible for me to write this book. Those were the people whom I met on the street who allowed me to walk beside them and experience their lives first hand. Without this experience I would be unaware of the seriousness of the social problems that plague us and are so threatening to the culture and lives of all Americans. Research through reading only skims the surface and many times is reported inaccurately.

This book is a work of nonfiction. Some names and identifying details have been changed to protect the privacy of those people.

About the Author

Marilyn Ribeiro has been a real estate broker and property manager for thirty-five years. Through her work she became known by many to be an advocate for inner city Americans as well as for the rights and safety of children. She lives in a suburb of Reading Pennsylvania with her husband Jack. Together they have three grown children and eight grandchildren.